COMMIT TO SIT

COMMIT TO $IT

TOOLS FOR CULTIVATING A MEDITATION PRACTICE

FROM THE PAGES OF *Tricycle: The Buddhist Review*

Foreword by Pema Chödrön

Preface by James Shaheen,
Tricycle Editor and Publisher

Edited by Joan Duncan Oliver

A *TRICYCLE* BOOK

HAY HOUSE, INC.
Carlsbad, California • New York City
London • Sydney • Johannesburg
Vancouver • Hong Kong • New Delhi

Published and distributed in the United States by: Hay House, Inc.:
www.hayhouse.com • **Published and distributed in Australia by:** Hay
House Australia Pty. Ltd.: www.hayhouse.com.au • **Published and
distributed in the United Kingdom by:** Hay House UK, Ltd.: www.
hayhouse.co.uk • **Published and distributed in the Republic of South
Africa by:** Hay House SA (Pty), Ltd.: www.hayhouse.co.za • **Distributed
in Canada by:** Raincoast: www.raincoast.com • **Published in India by:**
Hay House Publishers India: www.hayhouse.co.in

Design: Tricia Breidenthal
Photos on pages 24–33: copyright Warner Dick.
Reprinted with permission.

The author of this book does not dispense medical advice or pre-
scribe the use of any technique as a form of treatment for physical,
emotional, or medical problems without the advice of a physician, either directly or indirectly. The intent of the author is only to offer information of a general nature to help you in your quest for emotional
and spiritual well-being. In the event you use any of the information
in this book for yourself, which is your constitutional right, the author
and the publisher assume no responsibility for your actions.

Library of Congress Cataloging-in-Publication Data

Commit to sit : tools for cultivating a meditation practice / foreword
by Pema Chödrön, ; preface by James Shaheen ; edited by Joan
Duncan Oliver. -- 1st ed.
    p. cm.
"From the pages of Tricycle: the Buddhist review."
Includes bibliographical references.
ISBN 978-1-4019-2175-0 (tradepaper : alk. paper) 1. Meditation--
Buddhism. I. Oliver, Joan Duncan. II. Tricycle (New York, N.Y.)
BQ5625.C66 2009
294.3'4435--dc22

                 2008037882

ISBN: 978-1-4019-2175-0

12 11 10 09   4 3 2 1
1st edition, March 2009

FSC
Mixed Sources
Product group from well-managed
forests, controlled sources and
recycled wood or fiber
Cert no. BV-COC-930557
www.fsc.org
© 1996 Forest Stewardship Council

Printed in the United States of America

For all meditators
and aspiring meditators
everywhere

CONTENTS

PART III: MEDITATING WITH THE BODY

PART IV: EVERYDAY PRACTICE

PART V: OVERCOMING OBSTACLES

PART VI: STAYING WITH IT

OREWORD

Learning to Relax with the Truth

As human beings we have a very low tolerance for discomfort. But it is precisely at the place where we can't get comfortable that the journey to awakening begins.

We try all sorts of things to get rid of our uncomfortable feelings, without realizing that, in doing so, we are throwing away our wisdom. According to Vajrayana, or Tantric Buddhism, everything in us—particularly our strong emotions—is creative energy. So in trying to get rid of so-called negative feelings, it's as if we are throwing away our life force.

There is nothing inherently wrong with negativity. The problem is we never honor it. We never allow ourselves to know our negativity intimately, to smell it, taste it, touch it. Instead, we try to eliminate it by attacking others or punishing ourselves or repressing our feelings. But in between repression and acting out is something timeless, profound, and wise. When we can stay with discomfort, rather than try to eradicate it, the process of transmuting it begins.

Meditation is our support for learning to open to our discomfort. It gives us a way to move closer to our thoughts and emotions, a way to cultivate lovingkindness and compassion—the qualities of *bodhicitta*, the fully awakened heart and mind. When we begin to relate to ourselves without harshness or judgment or justification, meditation becomes a transformative process. We can finally let go of harmful patterns and experience unconditional joy.

Meditation is not just about feeling good, however. To think that is to set ourselves up for disappointment every time we sit. Even the most experienced meditator at times encounters physical pain and psychological turmoil. Buddhist practice is about diving into our real issues and befriending the deep-seated habitual patterns that keep us stuck in ignorance and confusion. In meditation, we come as we are. Complete acceptance of ourselves, with our passion, our aggression, our ignorance, and our sanity, is the essence of *maitri*—unconditional friendship with ourselves.

It is very healing to stop hiding from yourself. The Zen master Dogen Zen-ji said, "To know yourself is to forget yourself." Seeing ourselves clearly and honestly begins to dissolve the walls that separate us from others. Those walls—made of dogma and prejudice—arise out of our fear of knowing ourselves.

The technique of sitting meditation called *shamatha-vipashyana*—tranquility-insight—is a golden key to self-awareness. As we learn to relax with open-ended awareness, space opens up in our minds. We begin to notice gaps in our internal dialogue and to experience moments of clarity, of being right here, right now. Attending to our mind and body in the present is a way of being tender with ourselves—and with each other and the world. This quality of attention is inherent in the ability to love.

Meditation also strengthens our steadfastness with ourselves. Whatever arises—pain, boredom, sleepiness, wild thoughts or emotions—we learn to stay with it. We come to see that meditation isn't about attaining some ideal state. It's about being able to stay with ourselves, no matter what. Even longtime practitioners sometimes find themselves trying to use meditation as a way of escaping difficult emotions. But transformation comes only when we remember to move toward rather than away from our emotional distress. My teacher, Chögyam Trungpa Rinpoche, described emotion as a combination of energy and thoughts. Without our internal conversations, emotion can't proliferate. In meditation we learn to stay with the nonconceptual energy of the emotion, experience it fully, then leave it as it is, without adding fuel to the fire.

Waking up is a lot like giving up an addiction. We go through withdrawal symptoms, weaning ourselves from dependence on habitual, small-minded patterns of perception. Enlightenment means being fully awake, fully present, with no more need to hide out. Simply by staying present with the immediacy of our experience, we relax into the open dimension of our being. It is like stepping out of a fantasy and relaxing with the truth.

Letting go and relaxing into the open dimension of our being was the theme of a dharma talk I gave some years ago that appeared in the very first issue of *Tricycle*. I recalled watching ravens playing in the wind near my home on Cape Breton in Nova Scotia. The wilder the weather, the more the birds seemed to love it. They would cling to the tops of the trees, holding on with their claws and beaks, then let go and float away on the wind. Once, in a hurricane, I saw them clinging to each other's feet, then dropping off and flying out, like trapeze artists in a circus act. The birds, I observed, had had "to develop a zest for challenge and for life."

The whole journey of awakening is like that: we continually come up against challenges, then have to learn to soften and open to them. Meditation ultimately helps us say yes to life—and to play like a raven in the wind.

Pema Chödrön
Gampo Abbey

PREFACE

Tricycle: The Buddhist Review was launched in 1991 to bring Buddhist teachings and practices to the general reading public. In the years since, the magazine's editors have watched interest in meditation grow to include not only those in spiritual search but also those for whom a regular sitting practice has become an essential component of a healthy and meaningful life.

A few years back, we were pleased to discover that "Commit to Sit: *Tricycle's* 28-Day Meditation Challenge"—a special section developed by a young editor in our office—had inspired a good number of our readers to begin a daily meditation practice. Quite a few of them— newcomers and pros alike—also joined the online forum we set up as a supplement to the section. Online, the Meditation Challenge participants offered one another support, discussing the day-to-day challenges and rewards of contemplative practice. We soon realized that our simple challenge—so modest in its beginnings—had tapped into a need far more widespread than we had anticipated: doctors, educators, lawyers, nurses, housewives, and truck drivers were finding that the 28-day program had prompted them to ask questions about their lives that opened them to a whole new world of possibility. As the group grew, we invited meditation teacher Sharon Salzberg—who, along with Joseph Goldstein, had provided the daily meditation teachings and techniques in "Commit to Sit"—to join the online forum and offer guidance. We realized that there was a call for more instruction in Buddhist meditation and decided to mine the wealth of material in our archives and provide it.

With this book, *Tricycle* reviews editor Joan Duncan Oliver—a journalist and author who is a veteran of spiritual writing and practice—has brought together the broad range of meditative techniques that have appeared in the magazine over the years. Though targeted to the reader who would like to begin meditating, this collection also offers support and guidance to the longtime meditator who hopes to sustain a lifelong practice. In extending *Tricycle*'s mission into book form, Oliver has developed a guide to meditative practice for seekers wishing to deepen their understanding of themselves and their world.

One bit of advice I pass along from my own experience: as Thai Forest monk Thanissaro Bhikkhu—prolific translator, teacher, and frequent *Tricycle* contributor—has pointed out to me many times, meditation need not be the arduous pursuit it is to so many. "There is no reason for us to huff and puff," he says, "when we can *just breathe.*" Finding pleasure in our meditation practice is essential if we are to continue sitting with any regularity. So, with book in hand, sit back, pay attention, and breathe!

James Shaheen
Editor and Publisher
Tricycle: The Buddhist Review

$\mathcal{I}$NTRODUCTION

With all the emphasis today on meditation as a tool for health and well-being, it's easy to forget that it's something other than a means of relaxation. Studying Buddhist practices is a wonderful reminder that meditation is first and foremost the vehicle of our liberation—a tool for finding true happiness. Many of the meditative techniques Buddhists today engage in—including some you'll find in this anthology—can be traced back to practices the Buddha himself used for his own awakening and later taught to his followers.

The Buddha didn't invent meditation, but you might say he took mind training to another level. Like the Hindu and Jain masters of his time, he became adept at reaching ever higher bliss states. But rather than seeking to transcend reality, he wanted to understand it. Meditation allowed him to penetrate the nature of reality and the depths of the human mind and heart.

One reason the Buddha's teachings are so powerful for us today is that his approach was not faith-based but scientific: he discovered these truths through direct experience. The Buddha wasn't a god; he was an ordinary guy. Well, a prince of the warrior caste, actually, but a mortal one, named Siddhartha. At the age of 29, he had a crisis of meaning and went off in search of answers: Why was there so much unhappiness in the world? How could one find an end to all this pain and sorrow? He sat down—literally—in the middle of the problem, meditating intensely for the next six years. At the end of that time, he famously had a Great Awakening, rising from his meditation spot under a pipel tree—later called the Bodhi tree—as the Buddha, a name meaning "Awakened One." From his experiences in meditation the Buddha saw that the fundamental source of our discontent is not the circumstances of our lives but the workings of our minds—our false beliefs and misguided thoughts. He saw, too, that just as the mind is the source of our unhappiness and dissatisfaction, it is also the font of our salvation—of freedom from misery. In awakening the ordinary mind to Big Mind—to awareness of the true nature of things—we can find genuine happiness.

Because of his systematic exploration of how the mind gets us in—and out of—trouble, the Buddha is often called the world's first psychologist. Through his penetrating, experiential understanding he uncovered the essential facts of life: what he called the Four Noble Truths.

The First Noble Truth acknowledges that there is suffering or dissatisfaction (*dukkha* in Pali, the language of the earliest Buddhist texts). Life is difficult, in other words. The Second Noble Truth identifies the cause of suffering as craving and attachment—craving for what we want and attachment to what we have. Even when our desires are fulfilled, we aren't satisfied. But clinging to anything, even life itself, is futile. Everything changes, nothing lasts. All beings, without exception, eventually die.

There is hope, however. The Third Noble Truth says there's an end to suffering. Through clear seeing we can free ourselves from the endless cycle of craving and attachment, disappointment and loss. We see the folly of our greed, aversion, and delusion—our insatiable desire for what we want, our resistance to what we *don't* want, and our ignorance of the way life really is. The Fourth Noble Truth offers a way out of our predicament: the Noble Eightfold Path. This is the Buddha's blueprint for awakening to the joy of existence, based on his own experience. Meditation is but one of the three basic themes of the path; it works together with wisdom and ethical conduct to awaken us. Vajrayana teacher Judith Lief has described meditation as "not merely a useful technique or mental gymnastic but part of a balanced system to change the way we go about things at the most fundamental level."

Descriptions of the Eightfold Path generally begin with the wisdom section: right view and right intention. ("Right" here means "perfect" or "skillful.") Right view is seeing things as they really are. That includes grasping the three marks of existence: *dukkha*, suffering; *anicca*, the impermanence of all things; and *anatta*, or non-self. (Non-self doesn't deny your existence experientially—yes, there's a "you" reading this sentence. It means there's no permanently existing entity you can point to as "myself.") Right view also includes an understanding of *karma*, cause and effect. While the Buddha's contemporaries held a deterministic view of karma, his experience told him otherwise: the past shapes the present but the future is malleable, influenced by many factors, among them our present intentions and actions. Right intention, the other prong of wisdom, refers to the mental impetus behind our actions. Skillful intentions lead us toward awakening, unskillful intentions away from it.

The second theme of the Eightfold Path is ethical conduct, or virtue. In this section are right speech, right livelihood, and right action—skillful intentions manifesting in the world.

That brings us to meditation, the third theme of the Eightfold Path—and the theme of this book. In this category, we find right effort, right mindfulness, and right concentration. Right effort signifies the attitude, the mental energy behind our attempts, on the one hand, to prevent "unwholesome" mind states from arising or continuing and, on the other, to cultivate and maintain "wholesome" mind states. Right mindfulness refers to clear perception, right concentration to one-pointedness of mind.

●●● ● ●

Throughout *Commit to Sit* you will find references to the Dharma—the teachings of the Buddha. It's important to know, however, that you don't have to be a Buddhist to benefit greatly from the meditation practices set out in this book. The latest research by neuroscientists is demonstrating that these ancient techniques have salubrious effects on health, behavior, and mood. The technology of true happiness that the Buddha taught is now finding support in the modern lab. And the good news is this technology is accessible to us all.

Tricycle's aim has always been to present the Buddha's teachings as living dharma—teachings that can make a difference in our daily lives. The authors you will encounter in this book are contemporary teachers, many of whom are well known for introducing Buddhism to Westerners and to the mainstream. Their teachings arise not only from their grasp of the Dharma but also from the deep well of their own experience.

One of the most beloved of these teachers is Pema Chödrön, who wrote the Foreword to *Commit to Sit.* Born in America as Deirdre Blomfield-Brown, she was a wife and mother working as a schoolteacher before the pain of a second divorce led her to Tibetan Buddhism. She went on to take full ordination as a Buddhist nun and become abbot of Gampo Abbey in rural Nova Scotia. Since then, Pema has inspired many thousand Westerners with the essential promise of Buddhist practice: that each of us has within us the wisdom and compassion we need to break out of the prison of our own ignorance and confusion. Meditation is the key to knowing ourselves and removing the barriers that separate us from others.

If you are new to meditation—or to the teachings of the Buddha—you will probably want to begin at the beginning, with Part I, Getting Started. Here you will find not only a brief introduction to the purpose of meditation but also suggestions for finding a comfortable sitting posture and establishing a regular practice.

Part II, Meditation Basics, includes instructions on practices from the main traditions of Buddhism, including Theravada, or the Teachings of the Elders; Mahayana, primarily Ch'an/Zen; Vajrayana, most commonly known to us through Tibetan Buddhism; and Pure Land, a faith-based East Asian school. At the beginning of the section is "The Meditation Challenge." If you tried nothing else in the entire book, following the instructions in "The

Meditation Challenge" would give you a solid ground-ing in meditation. Based on a Sounds True audio course created by two well-known teachers, Sharon Salzberg and Joseph Goldstein, "The Meditation Challenge" sets out a comprehensive four-week program that introduces basic practices the Buddha taught and lays the founda-tion for ongoing practice. Other articles in Part II out-line the fundamentals of *shamatha* (concentration) and *vipassana* (insight) meditation; *metta,* or lovingkindness, meditation; *zazen,* Zen meditation; and *tonglen* (giving and taking), a Tibetan Buddhist practice to cultivate compassion. Plus, there's a guided meditation to awaken joy. "Worry Beads" walks the reader through a Pure Land practice of repeating the mantra of Amida Buddha—the Buddha of Everlasting Light—while fingering a *mala,* or string of prayer beads.

Not all meditation is sitting meditation. In addition to practices that center on awareness of sensations in the body, Part III, Meditating with the Body, introduces practices that focus on movement, including walking practice. Hatha yoga aficionados may be particularly interested in "Breath and the Body," which integrates meditative techniques and yogic postures for a deeper experience of both. For many Westerners, the ancient meditative practice of bowing will be a new experience. It is not necessary to complete the Tibetan Buddhist foundational practice of 100,000 prostrations to benefit from this expression of reverence and humility.

Ultimately, the point of meditation is not to become skilled at sitting on the cushion but to find inner freedom and a wiser, more compassionate approach to life. Part IV, Everyday Practice, sets out ways of practicing mind-fulness on the hoof, whether outdoors in nature, at the office, in the car, or at the dinner table. There are practices for cultivating generosity and patience and curbing the urge to gossip—all essential to the well-being of self and society. An interview with the respected Burmese master Sayadaw U Tejaniya includes thoughts on how Buddhist practice can relieve depression. The section closes with practices for growing through life's inevitable losses.

Meditation brings clarity, but it isn't always smooth sailing. The Buddha recognized such hindrances to practice as doubt, desire, anger, sloth, and restlessness—what modern psychologists might characterize as resistance. And even the most committed meditators go through dry spells when practice seems to be leading nowhere, and it's tempting to quit altogether. Part V, Overcoming Obstacles, deals with common frustrations and distractions. Pain in the back and legs are among the most prevalent obstacles meditators encounter. This section contains practical ways of handling both physical and emotional discomfort, including how to use chronic pain and desire as objects of meditation.

Once you've learned to meditate, begun a regular practice, and figured out how to deal with obstacles, then what? The challenge is continuing and deepening your practice. Part VI, Staying With It, includes wise advice from 21 experienced meditators on everything from sitting with others to changing your posture to having faith in the process. But in the end, meditation comes down to making a commitment to yourself. "The Joy of Effort" provides advice for strengthening your intention and refining your practice.

So, take what you can use from these pages. Try these practices. Make them your own. If you want to go deeper, you can join a sitting group or seek out a teacher.

"Be an island unto yourself," the Buddha said. Be your own refuge: you are the agent of your own salvation. But you are not alone. For nearly 2,600 years, meditators have found inspiration and guidance in what the Buddha taught and in the experiences of other meditators. With the practices in these pages, we invite you to do the same.

We also invite you to join *Tricycle*'s online *sangha*, or community of practitioners, at www.tricycle.com. Check out the resources listed there, and let us know your experiences with the practices in *Commit to Sit*.

PART I

GETTING STARTED

What is meditation? How do I begin a meditation practice? Where should I meditate? How long should I sit? What's the best posture to assume?

If you're new to meditation, you probably have questions like these. Even if you've been meditating for awhile, you may wonder at times if you're on the right track. In this section, Tricycle contributors answer questions on the nuts and bolts of meditation and offer suggestions to help you establish a regular sitting practice.

In "The Heart of Meditation," Lama Surya Das, a teacher in the Tibetan Buddhist tradition, discusses what meditation is—and isn't—then sets out an exercise ("Simply Being") to get you started.

"The Refuge of Sitting" and "Cultivating a Daily Meditation Practice" contain basic advice on such matters as when, where, and how long to sit and how to make meditation a regular habit.

Sitting cross-legged on a meditation cushion need not be torturous if you follow the suggestions in "Posture, Posture, Posture"—they're drawn from a traditional seven-point Tibetan Buddhist method for "taking your seat." However, even experienced meditators experience discomfort from time to time. Cyndi Lee, a yoga teacher who is a longtime Buddhist meditator, offers a sequence of yoga postures that takes only five minutes to complete but prepares both body and mind for meditation practice.

THE HEART OF MEDITATION

*Meditation is the path of awakening,
teaching us to be present and aware*

by Lama Surya Das

Meditation, simply defined, is a way of being aware. It is the happy marriage of doing and being. It lifts the fog of our ordinary lives to reveal what is hidden; it loosens the knot of self-centeredness and opens the heart; it moves us beyond mere concepts to allow for a direct experience of reality. Meditation embodies the way of awakening: both the path and its fruition. From one point of view, it is the means to awakening; from another, it is awakening itself.

Meditation masters teach us how to be precisely present and focused on this one breath, the only breath; this moment, the only moment. Whether we're aware of it or not, we are quite naturally present to this moment—where else could we be? Meditation is simply a way of knowing this.

Although most Westerners tend to conceive of Eastern forms of meditation as something done cross-legged with eyes closed, in a quiet, unlit place, the Buddha points with equal emphasis to four postures in which to meditate: sitting, standing, walking, and lying down. The *Maha-satipatthana Sutta* says: "When you sit, know that you are sitting; when standing, know you are standing . . ." This pretty much covers all our activities, allowing us to integrate meditative practice into daily life. Learn to sit like a Buddha, stand like a Buddha, walk like a Buddha. Be a Buddha—this is the main point of Buddhist practice.

While many people today practice meditation for physical and mental health, a deeper approach to practice energizes our inner life and opens the door to realization. In Tibetan, the word for meditation is *gom,* which literally means "familiarization" or "getting used to," and, in this sense, meditation is a means by which we familiarize ourselves with our mind. The common Pali term for meditation is *bhavana,* meaning "to cultivate, to develop, to bring into being." So we might then think of meditation as the active cultivation of mind leading to clear awareness, tranquility, and wisdom. This requires conscious effort.

Meditation is not about getting away from it all, numbing out, or stopping thoughts. Without trying to be rid of pesky thoughts and feelings, we learn how to practice being aware of them in the fleeting immediacy of the very moment in which they present themselves. We can cultivate awareness of any object: sounds, smells, physical sensations, perceptions, and so forth. Everything is grist for the mill—even those things we find terribly unpleasant.

Like the archer straightening his arrow and perfecting his aim, the practitioner of meditation straightens out the mind while aiming his or her attentional energy at its object. Learning to drop what we're doing, however momentarily, and to genuinely pay attention in the present moment, without attachment or bias, helps us become clear, just as a snow globe becomes clear when we stop shaking it and its flakes settle.

This settling process of concentrated attention has four stages: First, the letting go of distracting inner objects—such as feelings, thoughts, attractions, and aversions—and all outer objects; second, the attainment of serene one-pointedness of focus; third, the refinement of this state of concentration into a subtler and purer awareness. The fourth and final stage is the attainment of a state of simple wakefulness and equanimity conducive to clear vision and profound comprehension, an awareness beyond subject and object.

Let's take an example: In breath-awareness meditation—the technique known as mindfulness of breathing (*anapanasati* in Pali)—we first observe the breath by intently following the tiny movements and physical sensations associated with each in- and out-breath. When we are distracted, we simply bring the wandering mind back to the object of attention. (In this case it is the breath, but whatever the particular practice—mantra, visualization, and so forth—the principle is the same.) Then, gradually relaxing into the object, we notice the gentle tide of thoughts and feelings subside as we fine-tune our focus. Later, as our awareness deepens, we abandon any dualistic notion of inner and outer as we become the breath itself. This calls to mind the haiku master Basho's saying that in order to write about a tree, he would watch the tree until he became the tree. We watch the breath until we become the breath. In this way, as it is said in Zen, we come to know the breath, ourselves, and all things intimately.

In the beginning, concentration is key. Concentrative meditations, or *samatha* (*shamatha* in Sanskrit), are said to be the useful means but not the end. The stability of mind established by samatha becomes the foundation for insight meditation, or *vipassana* (*vipashyana* in Sanskrit), in which the critical faculties of mind discern the nature of *samsara*, the cycle of death and rebirth: impermanent, without self, and ultimately unsatisfactory.

There are many techniques for developing concentration and insight, but the point is to not be caught up in and overly influenced by the ever-running narratives and desires of the mind. All these techniques center on the vital principles of nonjudgmental openness and relaxation with applied and discerning awareness. As practice matures, effortless, innate wakefulness is balanced by the discipline of mindfulness. What we call "mindfulness meditation" can be broadly defined as any conscious activity that keeps the attention anchored in the present moment, allowing us to see clearly what is happening, to distinguish what is wholesome from what is unwholesome, and to perceive the interdependent working of things. In the *Satipatthana Sutra* the Buddha identified four basic foundations of mindfulness: the body, feelings (in the sense that all sense impressions feel pleasant, unpleasant, or neutral), mind states, and mental objects. Paying careful attention to these aspects of ourselves brings self-knowledge and wisdom.

Mindfulness is the tool we use to bring the mind back home, to the present moment, to what is, just as it is, and to who and what we actually are. Through mindfulness we learn how not to be so distracted by thoughts, feelings, memories—our running inner narrative.

Mindful awareness frees us from habitual patterns, opening up a space between stimulus and response, allowing us to consciously choose how to respond to things rather than blindly react. With the discernment of mindfulness we no longer fall prey to karmic habits and unwholesome conditioning. As the pioneering Zen master Shunryu Suzuki said, "We pay attention with respect and interest, not in order to manipulate but to understand what is true. And seeing what is true, the heart becomes free." This is not just Buddhist double-talk. In the *Diamond Sutra* the Buddha says of his enlightenment that he has obtained nothing that wasn't in him all along, there for the finding.

There are various Buddhist schools with different approaches and practices, but committed meditation practice is, in short, the way we apply the Buddha's final words: "Work out your own salvation with diligence."

In Tibetan Buddhism it is said that detachment is the root of meditation and devotion is its head. *Bodhicitta* (the aspiration to attain enlightenment for the welfare of others) is its soul. Mindfulness is its breath, vigilance its skin, and nondistraction its essence. Balance and harmony are the seat of meditation, and penetrating wisdom is its eye. Nowness is the time, and this place is the place. Self-discipline is the very bones of Buddha, and present-moment awareness is the heart of it all.

Milarepa said, "The ultimate view is to observe one's mind, steadfastly and with determination." When the Buddha stated, over 2,500 years ago, that anyone could become enlightened through applying his teachings, he meant it. And many have reaped those blessed results. This is the promise of Buddha-dharma, of the wisdom of meditation.

Excerpted from "The Heart-Essence of Buddhist Meditation," Vol. XVII, No. 2, Winter 2007

Guided Meditation: Simply Being

by Lama Surya Das

- *Sit comfortably and close your eyes or lower your gaze.* Take a deep breath or two and relax. Breathe slowly and let go, releasing all the tension in your body.

- *Stop doing and settle back into just being.* Let things settle without your direction or intercession. Open yourself to the wisdom of allowing, of inclusive acceptance. This is the inner secret to natural meditation.

- *Don't get lost.* Stay right here, at home and at ease. Befriend yourself; familiarize yourself with your own fundamental presence. Let awareness be uninterrupted by techniques or concepts.

- *If and when you feel lost, distracted, spaced out, or sleepy, get in touch with your breath.* Watch the breath; observe the inhalation and exhalation as they effortlessly occur. Feel the

breath moving in and out, anchoring you
in the present moment while you let everything go, without judgment, evaluation, or
interference.

- *Opening gradually to the effortlessness of pure
  presence, turn your attention inward.* All we
  seek can be found within. This is the process and practice of inner freedom. Enjoy
  the buoyant peace, harmony, and delight of
  natural meditation.

Adapted from "Guided Meditation: Simply Being," Vol. XVII, No. 2,
Winter 2007

THE REFUGE
OF SITTING

*dvice on developing a
disciplined meditation practice*

by Narayan Liebenson Grady

Developing a disciplined sitting practice is a matter of commitment and patience. For many practitioners, it is not easy, even for those who have been sitting for a while. Sitting every day must become a priority in our daily lives rather than just one more thing we have to do. Here are a few tips:

Plan to sit at the same time each day. One of the benefits of doing this is that one gets to know the mind that doesn't want to sit. Personally, I like to sit immediately upon waking up in the morning. For many people, this seems to be a good time, before we become engaged in the activities of the day. But if you have small children or a demanding job, this may not be possible. And some of us have rebellious natures, so any routine presents a problem. Then we need to be flexible.

Another common question is how long to sit. Generally it is better to sit for a shorter amount of time than to sit way beyond our capacity. We should determine for ourselves the amount of time we sit—there are no set formulas. Too long, and we may never want to sit again; too short, and our practice won't develop.

It can be helpful to set a timer rather than having to watch a clock. Because the practice is to let go of thoughts about the past and the future, this will free you from having to think or worry about time. You can simply set a specific amount of time to sit and rely on an external sound to signal when the sitting is over.

It is important to sit with the clear intention to be present. At the same time, we need to let go of expectations. In a very real sense, what happens when we sit is none of our business. The practice is to accept whatever arises instead of trying to control our experience. What we can control is our wise effort to be present with what is. We can spend a lot of our sitting time dwelling on memories of past sittings or fantasizing about those to come. When we read or hear about the benefits of meditation, it is tempting to dwell on the stories of wonderful outcomes instead of doing the work of actualizing these possibilities ourselves. There can be a big gap between what we have read and what is actually happening. Sitting is a way of putting our bodies behind our aspirations.

Some of us sit only when our lives are going well. When difficulties arise, we stop our practice rather than sit with disturbing emotions such as anxiety and anger. Others sit only when facing a big challenge, hoping that sitting will help us get through it. Being aware of these tendencies is part of what we face in sustaining a regular practice.

What hinders and intimidates beginners especially is experiences such as restlessness, sleepiness, and boredom. If we view these energies as part of the practice itself instead of what we need to get rid of in order to meditate, our sittings will be smoother, and we will develop the inner strength to be able to be with all experiences with greater equanimity.

Usually it is easier to sit for a longer amount of time in the company of others than to sit alone. Peer pressure can be a good thing. By sitting with others, even once a week, we reinspire our practice, while in sitting alone we learn self-reliance.

Whatever technique you are using, remember that the spirit of practice is more important than the technique. Finding a way to enjoy just sitting is key. Sitting meditation is a refuge, not a test.

Excerpted from "The Refuge of Sitting," Vol. XIII, No. 2, Winter 2003

CULTIVATING A DAILY MEDITATION PRACTICE

by Sharon Salzberg and Joseph Goldstein

Adapted by Alexandra Kaloyanides

The emphasis in meditation practice is on the word "practice." It's a lifelong journey, a process of learning to come back to clear, unobstructed experience. Checking in daily with this profound practice will yield the greatest impact throughout your life.

Just as painful habits take time to unravel, helpful habits take time to instill. Here are some suggestions to help you establish a daily meditation practice. None of these ideas is a hard and fast rule; try using them instead as tools to support your intention.

- *Plan to meditate at about the same time every day.* Some people find it best to sit right after they get up, while others find it easier to practice after a shower and coffee; your second practice could be in the afternoon or at bedtime. Experiment to find out what times work best for you.

- *Find a quiet place to meditate.* It could be in your bedroom or living room, in a basement or attic, or on a porch. Wherever you sit, pick a place where you can be relatively undisturbed during your meditation sessions. Try to keep your space free of clutter. If you can't dedicate this space exclusively to meditation, make sure you can easily carry your chair, cushion, or bench to and from it each day.

- *Bring inspiring objects to your meditation space:* an image, some incense, or possibly a book from which you can read a short passage before beginning.

- *Keep it simple.* The purpose of your practice is not to induce any particular state of mind but to bring added clarity to whatever experience you're having in the moment. An attitude of openness and curiosity will help you to let go of judgments, expectations, and other obstacles that keep you from being present.

Excerpted from "Commit to Sit," Vol. XVI, No. 3, Spring 2007; adapted from *Insight Meditation: A Step-by-Step Course on How to Meditate* with Sharon Salzberg and Joseph Goldstein, an interactive learning program from Sounds True

POSTURE, POSTURE, POSTURE

*ow to stay balanced and alert
while meditating*

by Sharon Salzberg and Joseph Goldstein

Adapted by Alexandra Kaloyanides

In the Buddhist tradition, mind and body are considered interdependent facets of our experience. A relaxed body helps relax the mind. The traditional meditation posture is designed to create a supportive physical structure for your awareness practice.

Many people experience some physical discomfort when they first begin sitting meditation. This is due partly to the unfamiliarity of the posture and partly to the practice of awareness itself, which may reveal more deeply held tension. We recommend that you sit comfortably and experiment until you find the posture that best supports your clarity and mindfulness.

If you sit on a chair, try not to lean your back against the backrest. Keep your spine as erect as possible without straining; your feet should be flat on the floor in front of you. Traditionally, Buddhist meditators have used a seven-point system to help them develop an optimal sitting posture on a cushion:

LEGS

Cross your legs loosely in front of you, at or just above the ankles. Your knees should be lower than your hips and resting on the ground. If your legs go to sleep during meditation, try crossing them the other way around—or you can sit with one leg in front of the other without crossing them at all. You can also kneel, turning your cushion on its side and placing it between your thighs and calves.

ARMS

Let your arms hang loosely at your sides. Now bend your elbows and let your hands fall naturally onto your thighs. Don't use your arms to support the weight of your torso or "hang on" to your knees to keep from falling backward. Some meditators prefer the so-called cosmic mudra, a gesture that is formed by cupping your right hand in your left, palms up, with the second knuckles of your right hand roughly aligned with the first knuckles of your left. The tips of your thumbs should just barely touch one another, forming a triangle with your hands. If you're feeling sleepy, it can be helpful to keep your thumbs slightly apart, so that they warn you of an imminent nap attack by colliding with each other. In this mudra, your hands are resting loosely in your lap, close to your belly.

BACK

How you hold your back is the most important element of your meditation posture. Imagine that your vertebrae are coins piled on top of one another. Let your back find its natural erectness; don't strain. You'll find that the innate concave curvature at the small of your back helps to support your weight. As one teacher has suggested, "Imagine that your spine is a strong oak tree. Now lean against it." Experiment with tipping your pelvis slightly forward and back to help find the natural curve of your spine.

EYES

Let your eyelids fall closed without squeezing them shut. If you find yourself dozing off, open your eyes slightly and let your gaze drop to the ground about six feet in front of you. Resist the temptation to let your eyes glaze, but at the same time, don't focus fiercely on whatever's in your field of vision. Let your gaze be soft.

JAW

Relax your jaw and mouth, with your teeth slightly apart. It's said that your lips should be parted enough to admit a grain of rice.

TONGUE

Let the tip of your tongue rest behind your upper front teeth. This reduces the flow of saliva and, hence, the urge to swallow.

HEAD AND SHOULDERS

When you first take your seat, position your head by gazing levelly in front of you. You'll find that this angles your neck very slightly forward. When you close your eyes, maintain this position. Be aware of your shoulders and keep them relaxed.

Excerpted from "Commit to Sit," Vol. XVI, No. 3, Spring 2007; adapted from *Insight Meditation: A Step-by-Step Course on How to Meditate* with Sharon Salzberg and Joseph Goldstein, an interactive learning program from Sounds True

YOGA FOR MEDITATORS

A *five-minute yoga regimen to enhance meditation practice*

by Cyndi Lee

photographs by Warner Dick

Who can say which comes first—a balanced body or a spacious mind? Science acknowledges that consciousness is not limited to the brain but is everywhere in the body. So the path to both steadiness and ease is consciously to unite body and mind. At the same time that yoga practice cultivates the physical stamina for meditation—that's where we get the steadiness—the practice of meditative awareness brings about ease of mind and heart.

The notion of union is at the heart of both hatha yoga and meditation practice. Yoga, from the Sanskrit *yuj,* to yoke or bind, refers to the union of apparent opposites: masculine and feminine energies, small mind and Big Mind, inner vision and outer awareness, steadiness and ease. We think of yoga as a balancing of mind and body. But where is the balance when your meditating body is so uncomfortable that instead of watching your thoughts arising and passing, your mind is totally focused on your aching back or knees?

As dharma practitioners, we know that everything changes, but sometimes emotional and physical disturbances—opinions, life experiences, digestive problems—lodge in the body, leading to blockages. Yoga practice consists of specific postures, or *asanas*—asana, in Sanskrit, means *seat* or *ground*—designed to ease the flow of breath, hormonal fluids, and blood and to release toxic buildup resulting from bad diet, stress, and lack of movement. Asana practice is also a profound way to process feelings. As the body moves, so do emotions. Breathing in and breathing out, carving space with our arms and legs, turning ourselves upside down, letting go of thoughts and returning to the breath—yoga practice allows our entire body-mind to stay fluid.

The yoga program on these pages is specifically designed for meditators. These postures will strengthen your back and abdominal muscles, create flexibility in your shoulders and hips, and make space for your internal organs to function better, as well as improve cardiovascular function and expand your breathing capacity. The entire program takes just five minutes and can be done at both the beginning and the end of your meditation. (In that way, it can serve as a bridge practice between sitting and moving mindfully through the world.) No warm-up or preparation is required. In fact, this *is* a warm-up. After a period of sitting, the program will get your *prana*—life force—moving again. Hold each pose for three to five breaths, except for the Cow and Cat poses.

COW POSE

Make sure your wrists are directly below your shoulders and your knees are directly below your hips. As you inhale, drop your belly and lift your sitting bones, chest, and face toward the sky. See if you can feel the front of your spine lengthening. Repeat this pose as many times as you want before moving on to Cat pose.

CAT POSE

As you exhale, tuck your head and tailbone under. Lift your belly up toward your spine, arching your back like a Halloween cat. Feel your back muscles soften outward. Repeat this pose as many times as you want. Cow and Cat create flexibility in your spine.

CHILD'S POSE

Separate your knees so that the space between them is wider than your hips. Press your pelvis back and drop your hips onto your heels. Rest your torso over your legs. Extend your arms in front of you. Tuck your head between them. This pose calms the brain, massages the abdominal and calf muscles, increases flexibility of the hips, and relieves lower-back tension.

SIDE STRETCH

Roll back up to a sitting position, taking time to feel each of the vertebrae as they stack on top of one another. Let your hips fall to the left. Lift your left arm and make a side bend to the right. Feel how your deep breathing opens up the accordion of your rib cage. If you feel like you're tipping over, put a cushion under your left hip. Come back to center. Now let your hips fall to the right and stretch your right side.

BOAT POSE

Swing your legs around in front of you. Keeping your back straight, balance on your sitting bones, bend your knees, and raise your legs. You can hold on to your thighs or extend your arms straight out in front of you. Eventually, try straightening your legs and reaching your toes toward the sky. This is a major abdominal strengthener to help support your back for long hours—or even ten minutes—of sitting.

TABLETOP POSE

With your knees directly over your ankles and your shoulders over your hands, press down into the earth with your hands and knees to lift your spine. Keep your back flat. Don't squeeze your bum, but use your leg muscles to support you. This pose strengthens your back, wrists, arms, and legs, increases flexibility in the shoulder area, and lengthens the quadriceps, the large muscles on the front of the thighs.

TWIST

Sit up straight with a tall spine. On an exhale, twist your body to the right. Release, switch arms, and twist to the left. This is one of the most beneficial postures. It massages the internal organs, helping digestion, and stretches the back muscles, relieving backaches, neck aches, and headaches.

STAR POSE

Bring your feet together, sole to sole, about two feet in front of you. As you exhale, slowly fold forward over your legs. Take your time, and don't worry about how far you bend. It's all about watching your body open up. If you keep paying careful attention as you do this pose, one day you'll notice that you're kissing your feet.

SHOULDER OPENER

Round up from Star pose and sit in a comfortable, cross-legged position. Use a cushion if you find it difficult to sit up tall on your sitting bones. It is important to keep your seat firmly grounded. As you reach the palms of your hands toward the sky, try to create length in your torso by lifting your ribs as your pelvis drops to connect with the earth.

SITTING TALL

Unifying heaven and earth, reach up with the crown of your head as you release your arms and let them float down. Rest your hands on your knees.

"Yoga for Meditators," from "The Body: Vehicle for Awakening," Vol. XII, No. 1, Fall 2002

PART II

MEDITATION BASICS

There are many ways to develop a meditation practice. The most important step is just to begin. All you need is willingness and an open mind. As the renowned Zen master Shunryu Suzuki said, "In the beginner's mind there are many possibilities, but in the expert's mind, there are few."

Some readers will want to dive in and take the 28-day challenge outlined in "The Meditation Challenge." Since it ran in the Spring 2007 issue, under the title "Commit to Sit," this has become one of Tricycle*'s most popular features ever. Thousands of readers have written letters to the magazine or posted messages on www.tricycle.com describing the transformative experience of following the steps of the four-week program. The program set out in "The Meditation Challenge" centers on basic teachings in the Vipassana tradition that trace back to the way the Buddha himself taught. They provide not only an excellent introduction to meditation but also a strong foundation for ongoing practice.*

Even if you decide not to accept the challenge in full or in part, you will find plenty of guidance in the rest of Part II. You can learn about vipassana, *or insight meditation ("Wisdom Arising") from Bhante Henepola Gunaratana, a Sri Lankan monk, and Sylvia Boorstein ("Focusing on the Breath"). Or about* zazen *("Zen, or Just Sitting") from Barry Magid, a psychotherapist and Zen teacher, and Martine Batchelor ("A Refuge into Being"). Gil Fronsdal offers instruction in* metta *(lovingkindness) meditation ("May We All Be Happy"), while Judith Simmer-Brown teaches* tonglen, *a Tibetan Buddhist practice for cultivating compassion ("Giving and Taking"),* and James Baraz offers a guided meditation for generating a feeling of well-being ("Awakening Joy").

And finally, you can find a good use for those "power beads" stuffed in the back of your bureau drawer. In "Worry Beads," Clark Strand explains the role of malas, or prayer beads, in Buddhist meditation and offers a practice, Saying the Nembutsu, from from the Pure Land tradition.

THE MEDITATION CHALLENGE

Take Tricycle's *28-day meditation challenge and go on retreat without leaving home*

by Sharon Salzberg and Joseph Goldstein

Adapted by Alexandra Kaloyanides

We don't have to remind you how toxic our lives can be. Stress at work, arguments with loved ones, poor diets, and too many hectic weekends conjure daydreams of Himalayan caves—guaranteed not to have cell phone reception. But in reality, even that retreat you've been planning for years feels like an impossible commitment.

Balancing a commitment to becoming more compassionate and wise with the responsibilities of a family, a career, and a checking account is a near-constant dilemma for many practitioners. To help, Tricycle teamed up with two of the West's foremost Buddhist teachers, Sharon Salzberg and Joseph Goldstein, to create an intensive meditation program designed for your busy schedule. No steep retreat fees, no putting newspaper delivery on hold, no out-of-office replies required.

Our 28-day challenge puts that daydream of an intense daily practice to the test. How different will you feel when you meditate every day for a month? What happens when you commit to the five traditional Buddhist vows for laypeople, including refraining from intoxicants and minding your speech? The meditation instructions provided here come out of the Vipassana tradition, which can be traced directly to the way the Buddha himself practiced. The program schedule is based on Vipassana retreats popular in the West and has been constructed to encourage and support your practice.

Whether you have months of retreat under your belt or have never been able to keep up a regular meditation practice, the simple structure of the program and accompanying instructions will help you to deepen and reinforce your practice. We have combined introductory teachings with guided meditations and a simple practice schedule so that anyone can participate in the challenge. However, people with an extensive daily regimen already in place may want to practice for longer periods than recommended or include elements from their regular practice.

Remember: This is a challenge. It is a structured four-week program intended to give you a taste of the benefits of intensive meditation training. Everyone will struggle to follow the program perfectly. Do not let missed meditation sessions or broken vows discourage you. Just return to the practice. As Sharon Salzberg often tells her students, it's the coming back that deepens our practice.

Alexandra Kaloyanides

GETTING STARTED

The Five Precepts

We begin our retreat by taking the five precepts, the principles that lay Buddhists have taken for over 2,500 years to express their commitment to everyday morality. We will make this commitment for the entire 28-day period. The precepts are simply training tools that help us to stay focused while we cultivate mindfulness. As many people on retreat have realized, the most purifying components of the experience are often the precepts. Our culture rarely provides us with occasion or motivation to relinquish alcohol for a month, and we all struggle with the consequences of the things we say. Taking 28 days to pay special attention to what goes into our bodies and what comes out of our minds is a rare opportunity to live in accordance with our ideals. The five precepts we undertake are expressions of our good-heartedness, our care for ourselves, and our care for others. Consider them skillful means designed as tools for practice, not markers for self-judgment.

- *The first precept is a commitment to refrain from killing or physical violence.* The idea is to use each day, each encounter, as an opportunity to express our reverence for life. This approach counters the tendency to feel separate and apart, objectifying other living beings to such an extent that we're actually capable of hurting them. The first precept includes all sentient beings—people as well as bugs and animals.

- *The second precept is a commitment to refrain from stealing,* or literally, as the suttas (sutras in Sanskrit)—traditional Buddhist texts—put it, "to refrain from taking that which is not offered or given." This means having a sense of contentment, being at peace with what we have, not taking more than we actually need, being grateful for what we have, and so on.

- *The third precept is refraining from sexual misconduct.* This means we resolve not to use our sexual energy in a way that causes harm or suffering to ourselves or others. When we don't know how to deal with our sexual desire in a skillful way, there are endless possibilities for abuse, exploitation, and obsession. The third precept includes not harming ourselves, in the sense that instead of being driven by our desires, we are able to make conscious choices.

- *The fourth precept is about using the power of speech in an ethical way.* Traditionally, we commit to refrain from lying, but actually this precept also covers harsh divisive speech and idle chatter. We recognize that our speech does, in fact, have tremendous power. Words don't just come out of our mouths and disappear. Rather, they are a very important means of connecting and have lasting effects and consequences. We need to be mindful of how we speak.

- *The fifth precept is a commitment to refrain from taking intoxicants that cloud the mind and cause heedlessness,* meaning drugs and alcohol (but not prescription medication). This precept is a traditional way of detoxifying our bodies and minds, but adhering to it can be challenging at social events where alcohol is considered a means of social connection and relaxation. However, if we are dedicated to maintaining this commitment, these situations often prove to be less awkward than we had feared, and the benefits of keeping the vow turn out to be even more fruitful than we had hoped.

When you find that somehow you have broken a precept, the important thing is to take it again. Castigating yourself, or seeing the broken precept as evidence of failure or an irredeemable character flaw, is pointless and counterproductive. Instead you might see the beauty and joy in living in harmony and use that inspiration to repair the fabric or wholeness in your life.

Meditation Practice

People have practiced some form of meditation, or quieting the mind, since the beginning of recorded history. All major world religions (and many lesser-known spiritual traditions) include some contemplative component. Vipassana, the type of meditation included in this program, is characterized by concentration and mindfulness. Also known in West as "insight meditation,"

COMMIT to SIT

vipassana meditation is designed to quiet the mind and refine our awareness so that we can experience the truth of our lives directly with minimal distraction and obscuration.

The practice of Buddhist meditation can be said to be nontheistic, that is, not dependent on belief in an external deity. Buddhism simply reflects back to us that the degree of our own liberation is dependent on the extent of our own effort. So the Buddha's style of meditation is compatible with any spiritual path, whether theistic or nontheistic. The practice of mindful awareness is an invaluable tool to anyone seeking spiritual awakening, mental clarity, or peace of mind.

The first pillar of meditation is concentration. Concentration is the development of stability of mind, a gathering in and focusing of our normally scattered energy. The state of concentration that we develop in meditation practice is tranquil, at ease, relaxed, open, yielding, gentle, and soft. We let things be; we don't hold onto experiences. This state is also alert; it's not about getting so tranquil that we just fall asleep. It's awake, present, and deeply connected with what's going on. This is the balance that we work with in developing concentration.

The other main pillar of meditation is the quality of mindfulness. That means being aware of what is going on as it actually arises—not being lost in our conclusions or judgments about it or our fantasies of what it means. Rather, mindfulness helps us to see nakedly and directly: this is what is happening right now. Through mindfulness we pay attention to our pleasant experiences, our painful experiences, and our neutral experiences—the sum total of what life brings us.

There are five guided meditations in this meditation challenge that give specific instructions for developing

44

the skills of concentration and mindfulness. The techniques they suggest are meant to be read, considered, and then gently and intentionally implemented into meditation periods.

WEEK ONE: THE BREATH

For the first week, our main focus is the breath. Awareness of the breath is the fundamental technique of insight meditation. By focusing our attention on our inhalations and exhalations we calm the mind and create the conditions for insight to arise. Twice a day this week we will meditate for 20 minutes, focusing on our breath. The following guided meditation will introduce you to this most basic and important practice.

Guided Meditation: Breathe Easy

In breath meditation, the mind can be relaxed and spacious; we don't have to fabricate anything. Take a few deep, easy breaths and release them. Allow the breath to become natural so you're not trying to force or control it in any way. Notice the place where you feel the breath most distinctly. It may be the in-and-out movements of the air at the nostrils. You may feel tingling or vibration or changes in temperature. You may feel the breath most distinctly with the rising and falling of the chest or the abdomen: stretching . . . pressure . . . tension . . . release. Wherever you feel it is the most natural, most easy, allow your mind to rest in that place and feel the breath. As you feel the breath, you can make a silent mental note to sharpen the concentration: "in" as you feel the breath go in; "out" as you feel it leave your body. Or "rising, falling" with the sensation in your chest or belly. Very gently, very quietly in your mind, just support the awareness of the actual sensations. You don't need to make the breath special. It doesn't have to be long or different from however it is, however it changes. It's happening anyway, so simply be aware of it, one breath at a time.

You may feel your attention wandering. You may realize that you've been lost in thought, planning, remembering, whatever. Perhaps it's been quite some time since you last felt the breath consciously. It doesn't matter. You don't have to judge or analyze or try to figure out how you've gotten to where you are. Don't worry. See if you can gently let go of whatever the distraction has been and simply begin again. Gently let go and return the attention to the actual feeling of the breath. This act of beginning again is the essential art of meditation practice; over and over and over, we begin again. You may find your attention wandering constantly. It doesn't matter. The mind has been trained to be distracted. In a very relaxed and patient manner, just let go, reconnect, come back to the feeling of the breath in this very moment, the natural, uncontrived, normal breath. You don't have to worry about the breath you've just taken, or the very next one to come. There's no comparison, no anticipation—it's the breath right in this moment, as it's happening. You can settle the mind there. Feel it. Don't try to hold on to the breath. You may discover that there's a pause or a gap between the in-breath and the out-breath or between the out-breath and the next in-breath. If you find such a pause, you can allow the attention to settle in the body. Simply feel your body sitting there. Then allow the next breath to come naturally. End the session by gently opening your eyes. Listen to sounds, feel your body, and see if you can bring some of this quality of presence and connection to the next activity you perform in the day.

Monday–Friday: Meditate for 20 minutes in the morning and in the evening, focusing on the breath.

Weekend Challenge: Devote two hours this weekend to contemplation of the breath. Sessions should be at least 30 minutes long. Spend the entire two hours in silence, alone or with other practitioners.

WEEK TWO: THE BODY

This week we will continue to work with the breath and begin to incorporate other sensations in the body into our meditation practice. For this second week, you are asked to meditate for 20 minutes twice a day and to practice walking meditation for 20 minutes once a day. Instructions follow for working with sensations in the body during seated meditation and for walking meditation.

Working with Pain

We can develop the liberating gift of relating skillfully to physical pain. It is important to learn how to open to pain because how we relate to pain in meditation is symptomatic of how we relate to all the unpleasant things in our lives.

The Buddha reminded us of a great and obvious truth when he taught that being born results inevitably in growth, decay, and death. If we have a body, we can be certain that at times we will also have pain and illness, and we know for sure that our body will die. Much of meditation practice is opening to this reality in a very immediate way—not merely thinking about it but experiencing it directly and deeply.

When physical pain predominates in your practice, you can try different strategies of awareness. First, notice the general area of sensation, for example, the knee or back. Simply be aware of the whole area, letting your mind relax and settle into the physical sensations. Second, observe precisely the particular nature of the sensations. Do you feel burning, pressure, searing, tightness, piercing, twisting, or some other variant of bodily feeling? Noting the particular quality of what you feel will help your mind to become more concentrated.

After you recognize what is actually there, the third step brings you even deeper. Allow your awareness to pinpoint the area of greatest intensity. Notice what happens. Usually the sensation—either pain or discomfort—will change in some way, and the point of intensity will shift. Then move your attention to that point and then to the next—something like "connecting the dots" of intensity.

When your mind becomes tired, come back to awareness of the whole area or even back to your breath. It is usually better to go back and forth between the breath and the pain for intervals of several minutes at a time because our mind has a tendency to pull back, become tired, and lose focus during long periods of intense unpleasant feeling. Unless we work skillfully with pain, it can exhaust us, and then mindfulness and energy decrease. Alternating between the breath and the pain keeps us more alert and energetic.

The value of altering our relationship to pain goes far beyond how and where we sit. Times of discomfort teach us how to practice freedom in all those life situations that make us uncomfortable. How are we relating just now, in this moment, to discomfort, pain, not getting what we want? It will be interesting to see, over and over again, how in those situations we think are intolerable, it is often our own resistance that makes them intolerable. The problem lies not in the situations but rather in our inability to just be with them, to just open to them.

But we also need to recognize our limits in certain situations. Sometimes experiences are too overwhelming to open up to all at once. We may need to back off for a while or to approach them gradually. Learning this balance is the key to so much of our practice. How much can we accept in a soft and gentle way before we close off, before we say, "This is too much"? Extending our limits makes us strong. Through this simple practice we develop a power of mind, a great capacity to be with painful situations. That strength transforms how we live our life.

This week, practice working with sensations in this way. Although pain is generally the type of sensation that cries the loudest for attention, it is also beneficial to learn to experience pleasant sensations in this direct way. Sometimes this is even more challenging, as it is so easy to become lost in the pleasant.

Guided Meditation: Walk the Walk

Walking meditation is the application of bare attention in movement. It becomes a model for being mindful in all the movements we make throughout the day.

Find a place, inside or outside, about 10 or 20 steps in length. Stand at one end of this path for a moment and settle the attention in the body with a body scan—the practice of sending your attention to every part of your body, starting on one end and moving all the way through to the other.

We'll divide the walking period into three sections. During the first section, walk back and forth at a slightly slower-than-normal speed. As you're doing this part of the walking practice, you can use a very simple mental label with each step. Note "left, right, left, right" or "stepping, stepping" each time the foot touches the ground.

The primary emphasis in the practice is to stay centered in the body, feeling the actual sensations of movement. The mental noting should be very soft, in the background. Use it simply as a way of helping to keep the mind connected to what's going on.

As you're walking at near-normal speed, feel the movement of your body. Feel the movement of the legs and the feet. Be relaxed in your body with the quality of bare attention. It's alert, it's receptive, it's noticing the sensations in the movement of walking.

Notice when your mind wanders. When you notice that you are lost in a thought, simply be aware of this and come back to the step.

After walking back and forth at a speed just a little slower than normal for about 10 minutes, begin to slow down. Now we'll divide the step into two parts. Begin to note the lifting and placing, lifting and placing. Feel the specific sensations associated with each of those parts of the step. As you lift, what is it that you feel in the foot and leg? As you place, what sensations are arising? See how carefully you notice what is going on—"lift, place, lift, place." Or you might note "up, down, up, down." Feel the specific sensations with each part of those steps.

After some time, slow the walking practice down even further. Now you can divide the step into three parts: "lift, move, place" or "up, forward, down." Finish one step completely before lifting the other foot. Settle back into the very slow and easy rhythm, with careful attention to the sensations of lifting, the sensations of moving forward, and the sensations of lowering the foot and touching.

The rhythm of this slow walking is quite different from the way we usually move. It may take a short while for you to get used to this rhythm, where you finish one step completely before lifting the other foot. Continue at this speed, settling back into the movement, settling into your body with bare attention, feeling the subtlety of sensations with each part of the step. Try to keep the mind and body relaxed. There need not be any kind of struggle or forcing.

Feel free to experiment with the speed at which you move, keeping in mind that the guideline is mindfulness. For most people, this means starting at a somewhat faster pace and then gradually slowing down as the mind becomes more focused and concentrated. If you find that the mind is wandering a lot, you can change the speed to a faster pace.

Generally, you place the emphasis on the sensations in the foot and leg as you move. At times, though, you can also be with the sensations of the whole body. Feel the whole body as it moves through space.

Sometimes in the evening, if you're feeling full of energy or restless and tired, you might find that walking practice is actually more helpful than sitting. Because the movement is quite obvious and tangible, people often find it easier to focus their attention in the walking. If you are struggling in your seated meditation periods in the evenings, feel free to replace them occasionally with periods of walking meditation.

Monday–Friday: Continue practicing seated meditation for 20 minutes in the morning and in the evening. This week, add a 20-minute walking meditation session each day.

Weekend Challenge: Devote three hours this weekend to contemplation on the body in sessions of at least 30 minutes. Spend a minimum of one hour practicing walking meditation. If you are able to practice for three solid hours, try alternating between seated and walking meditation in 30-minute periods with one half-hour break for tea. During breaks, maintain silence if possible and move carefully without rushing, paying special attention to the sensations in your body.

WEEK THREE: EMOTIONS AND HINDRANCES

Halfway there! Until now, you have been experiencing emotions and hindrances during your meditation periods, but the instructions have been to focus on the breath and the body. This week you will devote more attention to these emotions and hindrances and become more skillful in dealing with them. In order to do this, we investigate the nature of these experiences as they happen. This week, as your daily time commitment increases to two 30-minute meditation sessions and two walking periods, you will continue to work with the breath and the body while putting particular attention on emotions like anger and hindrances like restlessness. The following guided meditations provide instructions for working with the hindrances and emotions.

Guided Meditation: Handling Hindrances

The five classical hindrances to meditation practice are desire, aversion, sleepiness, restlessness, and doubt. One of the keys to a skillful relationship with the five hindrances is being able to name them or make a mental note of them. We practice noting very softly, giving about 95 percent of our attention to actually being with the experience, to sensing it completely. Only 5 percent of our energy goes into the soft, gentle naming of it.

We use mental noting with the hindrances to bring us into a direct relationship with them, as opposed to elaborating or judging or creating a story about what's going on. If aversion, or anger, arises, for example, we note it as "anger, anger." This brings us close to the exploration of anger itself. What is anger? What does it feel like? What is its nature?

Mental noting takes us in a very different direction from getting lost in a story, "Oh, this anger is so miserable; I am such a terrible person because I'm always angry; this is just how I will always be," and so on. Instead, we simply say to ourselves, "anger, anger" and cut through all of that elaboration, the story, the judgment, the inter-pretation.

As you note the particular hindrance, you can also be conscious of what happens to it. How does it behave? Does it intensify? Does it fade away? Pay particular attention to whether or not it manifests in the body. If so, how does it feel? What parts of the body are affected by the arising of this force in the mind? The chest, the stomach, the head, the eyes, the breath—where are you feeling it?

What does it feel like in the mind, in the heart, as a mood, as a coloration, as an experience? Do you feel open or do you feel contracted when this hindrance is present? Do you feel closed off and separate, or do you feel connected? Whatever it is, explore and discover without judgment. Simply pay attention. Watch and see the nature of this hindrance in the moment and observe how it changes. Is it growing stronger? Is it growing weaker? Is it changing into something else?

Listen to the voices that come along with the hin-drances. What are they saying to you? What are they saying about you and what you're capable of? Very often with the hindrances, and especially with the forces of desire or anger, we get so lost in the object that we forget to pay any attention to the feeling itself. We fixate so much on what we want or what we want to keep or what we hate and want to push away that we don't spend much time feeling the nature of desire or of anger itself. So ask yourself now, *What do they feel like?* See if you can let go of that fixation on the object of the feeling. Relax. Abide in the feeling. It's an act of discovery. It's as though somebody were to say to you, "What is desire?

What is anger?" Not "Why are you feeling it?" or "Is it right or is it wrong?" Just "What is it?"

The hindrances are going to arise. We don't have to be upset or afraid about that. We don't have to feel disappointed because of it. We can come to understand a great deal about our experience—about our own suffering and our release from suffering—just from coming to understand these hindrances better.

Guided Meditation: How Does It Feel?

We've talked about working with the mind states of the hindrances as they arise in meditation and in our lives. We also want to become aware of the entire range of emotional life. The various emotions that arise in sitting practice and in walking—we want to bring this awareness to all of these and then, beyond that, to the emotions we experience in the world every day. As you sit, feeling the breath, feeling sensations, noticing the hindrances as they arise, be aware of different emotions as they appear in your experience. There might be the feeling of happiness or sadness; there might be the feeling of joy or depression. You might feel quite light or buoyant. You might feel heavy or despairing.

Each one of these states can be opened to, noticed, and noted. The practice is to be aware of them without identifying with them—not taking them to be "I" or "self " or "mine" but seeing them as a constellation of experience arising out of conditions. We see them lasting for some time, changing, disappearing in the form of sensations in the body or particular thoughts or images associated with the emotion or as a certain texture or coloration of the mind. Each emotion has its own particular flavor, the flavor of sadness or happiness or joy or love or anger. We want to investigate all of these aspects.

The first step in working with an emotion is to recognize what it is. It's very helpful to use mental noting to bring forth clear recognition, *this is happiness, this is sadness, this is loneliness, this is excitement, this is interest, this is boredom.* Clear recognition can be very helpful. If other thoughts rush in to associate with the naming, practice returning again and again to the simple naming.

When an emotion is arising strongly in your experience, it's useful to notice the different aspects or constituents of the emotion. Feel the specific sensations in the body. Is there heat? Is the body contracted? Is it open? Is it soft? Notice whether there are particular images or thoughts associated with the emotion, and notice the "mind flavor" of the particular feeling. Open to the subtleties in the mind and body as each of these feelings arises.

Sometimes you may not be able to recognize exactly what the emotion is. There's no need to spend a long time trying to analyze it; you can simply open to the feeling with the general note of "feeling" or "emotion" until what it is becomes clearer to you.

So the first step is recognition. The second step is acceptance. There's often a tendency to resist or deny certain emotions, particularly if they're unpleasant. There are certain emotions that we don't like to feel. These can be different for each of us. For some people, there is a resistance to feeling anger or sadness or unworthiness. In our meditation practice, we want to recognize what's arising and be accepting of whatever it is. Acceptance is the key to the third step, which is nonidentification with the emotion. The understanding is that this constellation of experience is arising out of conditions and then passing away. It is nonpersonal. There's no one behind the emotion to whom it is happening.

This may take some practice to understand. It's a very subtle and difficult point because often what we most personalize, what we most identify with, are the emotions. They're what we're most likely to take ourselves to be.

Monday–Friday: Practice seated meditation for 30 minutes in the morning and in the evening. Include two periods of walking meditation, of any length, in the course of the day. Pay particular attention to emotions and hindrances, working with them according to the instructions above.

Weekend Challenge: Devote four hours this weekend to silent meditation in sessions of at least 30 minutes. Practice being mindful of emotions and hindrances as they arise this weekend, both during and outside of your formal meditation periods.

WEEK FOUR: THOUGHTS

You've made it to the final week. Acknowledge your hard work and recognize the joy that comes from following through on a commitment. In this final week we will further develop the skills we have worked on over the last 21 days and will expand our realm of focus to include thoughts.

Working with Thoughts

For the purpose of meditation, nothing is particularly worth thinking about: not our childhood, not our relationships, not the great novel we always wanted to write. This does not mean that thoughts will not come. In fact, they may come with tremendous frequency. We do not need to fight with them or struggle against them or judge them. Rather, we can simply choose not to follow the thoughts once they have arisen. The quicker we notice that we are thinking, the quicker we can see thought's empty nature.

Our thoughts are often seductive, and meditation may pass quickly when we sit and daydream; before we know it, the hour has passed. It may have been an enjoyable sitting, but it was not meditation. We need to be aware of this sidetrack in practice and remember that the kind of wisdom we want to develop comes intuitively and spontaneously from silent awareness.

Although meditation is not thinking, it can be clear awareness of thinking. Thought can be a very useful object of meditation. We can turn the great power of observation onto thought in order to learn about its inherent nature, becoming aware of its process instead of getting lost in its content.

In dharma teaching we speak frequently about the powerful impact of identifying with phenomena. Identification imprisons us in the content of our conditioning. One of the easiest ways to understand this imprisonment is to observe the difference between being lost in thought and being mindful of it.

The Buddha said that we are shaped, created, and led by our thoughts. If he was right, then it is important for us to watch our thought process closely to see where we get hooked, where we are seduced through identification into creating something that brings us unhappiness. It is amazing to observe how much power we give unknowingly to uninvited thoughts, *do this, say that, remember, plan, obsess, judge.* They can drive us quite crazy, and they often do!

The kinds of thoughts we have and the impact they have on our destiny depend on our understanding of things. If we are in the clear, powerful space of just seeing thoughts arising and passing, then it does not matter what species of thinking appears in the mind; they are all essentially empty of any substance at all, and we can see them for the passing show that they are. These all-powerful movers and shakers of the world that create us and lead us become little energy blips in our mind, with hardly enough power to create even a ripple. They seem like transparent dewdrops evaporating in the sun.

But there are many times when we are not simply watching thoughts come and go, either because we are lost in them or because we choose to think something through, perhaps as a precursor to action. In both cases it is crucial for us to discern wholesome from unwholesome thoughts in order to know which to give our energy to because these thoughts do have karmic impact—they lead us. From thoughts come actions; from actions come all sorts of consequences. Which thoughts will we invest in? Our great task is to see them clearly, so we can choose which to act on and which simply to let be.

It takes a great deal of alertness to stay aware of thoughts. They are extremely slippery. If you watch them in one place, they sneak in from another. But as practice evolves, two liberating things happen. First, our mind actually becomes quieter. Instead of being a rushing torrent, thoughts come less frequently, and we enjoy an increasing sense of calm and inner peace. Second, our observing power becomes quicker and stronger. We can see thoughts much more clearly and are taken for fewer unconscious rides. Without identifying with thoughts and giving them power, our mind abides in a natural state of ease, simplicity, and peace.

Guided Meditation: Counting Thoughts

As you sit, resolve to concentrate on the thought process for five minutes. Let your mind appear as a blank screen and watch carefully for thoughts to arise. They may come as images or words in the mind or both together. Some thoughts may arise with a feeling or physical sense as well. Note experience as it appears.

For five minutes, experiment with counting your thoughts. After noticing and counting the thoughts, simply wait, looking at the blank screen, for the next one to arise. Remember that some thoughts are very subtle, like *It's so quiet in here.* We count the thoughts not to form a judgment about ourselves and how much (or little) we think but to observe the thought process with mindfulness, without getting lost in each story. Can you describe your experience?

Carefully note each breath as "breath." As thoughts arise, note them simply as "not-breath." This also helps us cut our dualistic fixation with the content of our thoughts. Whether lovely or frightening, they are all noted simply as "not-breath." What kinds of thoughts predominate in your mind—words or pictures, those arising with a kinesthetic sense, or a combination?

If images are arising, can you note them as "seeing" and notice whether they are growing brighter, fading, breaking apart, moving closer, or staying just the same? Can you note the particular kind of thought, such as "planning," "remembering," "judging," "loving"?

Observe the effect of various types of thoughts—for example, of a future-directed thought like *I'm never going to get any better.* What happens to your mood, to your body as a consequence of this thought? What is the difference between simply observing it and getting lost in it?

Can you name an insistent thought with a label that reflects some compassion and humor? We call them the Top Ten tapes because they arise in the form of conditioned tapes in the mind. They play like songs on the radio, reflecting the same themes over and over again. Try giving them appropriate labels like "the Martyr tape," "the I-Blew-It-Again tape," "the Fear-of-the-Dark tape." Be lighthearted about these labels. We can see these tapes as conditioned forces and don't have to take ourselves so seriously. The repeated forces in the mind can be greeted in a friendly and openhearted way, *Oh, it's you again, Mad-Scientist tape. Hello.*

If a particular thought seems to be returning a lot, expand your field of attention to notice whatever emotional state may be feeding it. Unseen feelings are part of what brings thoughts back again and again. For example, anxiety often fuels future planning. At first the emotions may be half-hidden or unconscious, but if you pay careful attention, the feelings will reveal themselves. Use the sensations in the body to help guide the attention to whatever emotions may be present. You may find that watching tension in the chest uncovers sadness. Begin to note whatever emotions you see as a way of acknowledging them.

If there is a repeated physical pain or difficult mood, expand your field of attention to the thoughts, stories, or beliefs that may be feeding the difficult situation. When we are mindful, we may find a subtle level of self-judgment or a belief about our unworthiness, such as *I'm not as good as others. I'll always be this way.* These thoughts actually help perpetuate pain or unhappiness.

Monday–Friday: Increase your seated-meditation commitment to 45-minute sessions in the morning and in the evening. Also include two periods of walking meditation, of any length, in the course of the day.

Weekend Challenge: Devote one full day (from sunrise to sunset) to silent contemplation on the body, the feelings, and the mind. Create a schedule of alternating periods of seated and walking meditation with short breaks in the morning and afternoon and one two-hour lunch break. During break periods, move carefully, paying special attention to sensations in the body and activity in the mind. This is a good opportunity to learn how to take your mindfulness practice off the cushion and into your everyday life.

YOU'VE DONE IT!

Congratulations on completing the 28-day meditation challenge. But don't stop here. The challenge now is to incorporate your newly cultivated wisdom, peace, and diligence into your busy life. Reflect on your efforts this month, and think about how the process has unfolded for you in ways both expected and unexpected. Can you sense any change in your thought patterns and quality of attention? What commitments to meditation practice and ethical conduct would you like to keep? Take what you have learned about the practices and yourself and formulate a daily practice that works for you, and if you're still feeling adventurous, look into other kinds of retreats you might like to try. Visit www.tricycle.com for links to retreat centers, forums to share your experience with fellow retreatants, and advice from teachers on how to continue to develop your hard-earned concentration and tranquility.

Excerpted from "Commit to Sit," Vol. XVI, No. 3, Spring 2007; adapted from *Insight Meditation: A Step-by-Step Course on How to Meditate* with Sharon Salzberg and Joseph Goldstein, an interactive learning program from Sounds True

WISDOM ARISING

Training the mind's eye with
vipassana, or insight meditation

by Bhante Henepola Gunaratana

Vipassana, or insight meditation, is a way of training the mind to see things in a very special way as they happen. Seeing without using eyes is a special way of seeing. We train the mind to use our innate wisdom without using words, concepts, logic, or interpretation. In this training, concentration and mindfulness are united. Then wisdom arises and disintegrates what appears to be integrated. Our wisdom eye registers the constant flux of events that is taking place in every moment in our lives. Although this unbroken flux of events is what life is, one cannot be fully aware of this truth without paying attention to what is happening to one's mind and body every waking moment. With developed insight, our mind can be fully aware of the evolving, processing, and dissolving of everything that happens to us.

So we train the mind to see things as they happen, neither before nor after. We participate in what is happening and at the same time observe it without clinging to the events of the past, the future, or the present. We experience our ego or self arising, dissolving, and evaporating without leaving a trace of it. We see how our greed, anger, and ignorance vanish as we see the reality in life. Mindfully we watch the body, feelings, sensations, perceptions, and consciousness and experience their dynamic nature.

Watching impartially opens the mind to realize that there is no way to stop this flux even for a fraction of a second. We experience the freshness of life. Every moment is a new moment. Every breath is a fresh breath. Every tiny little thing is living and dying every fraction of a second. There is no way that we can see these momentary existences with our eyes. Only when the mind is sharp and clear, without the clouds of craving, hatred, and confusion, can it be fully aware of this phenomenon. When we don't try to cling to these experiences, we experience great joy, happiness, and peace. The moment we try to cling to any part of our experience—however pleasant or peaceful—joy, peace, and happiness disappear. The very purpose of vipassana meditation is to liberate the mind from psychic irritation and enjoy the peace and happiness of liberation. Nevertheless, if we cling to peace or happiness, these feelings vanish instantaneously. This is a very delicate balance that we should maintain through the wisdom that arises from vipassana meditation.

"Wisdom Arising," from "Five Practices to Change Your Mind," Vol. XIV, No. 4, Summer 2005

FOCUSING ON THE BREATH

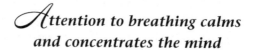

*Attention to breathing calms
and concentrates the mind*

by Sylvia Boorstein

As a way of beginning, we have people bring their attention to the breath. But really, if you think about it, is there such a thing as "the breath"? There are vibrations and pulsings and pullings; there are all kinds of sensations that make up this thing called "the breath," but there isn't any one thing that makes up "the breath." That's a name we give to a very complex variety of body sensations. And even when we begin to practice for the very first time, when we close our eyes for the first five minutes, there is such a lot of dharma to learn. One sits down, closes one's eyes, and sees that there is a lot going on! Isn't it true that there are twitchings and pulsings that you weren't aware of?

If you pay attention for just five minutes, you know some very fundamental dharma: things change, nothing stays comfortable, sensations come and go quite impersonally, according to conditions, but not because of anything that you do or think you do. Changes come and go quite by themselves. In the first five minutes of paying attention, you learn that pleasant sensations lead to the desire that these sensations will stay and unpleasant sensations lead to the hope that they will go away. And both the attraction and the aversion amount to tension in the mind. Both are uncomfortable. So in the first five minutes, you get a big lesson about suffering: wanting things to be other than what they are. Such a tremendous amount of truth to be learned from just closing your eyes and paying attention to bodily sensations.

So then why, if all the myriad body sensations are so important, spend so much time bringing the attention back to the breath? Especially when people come to me and say, "I have a lot of trouble staying with the breath." If I now say that the breath is merely one of many different bodily sensations, why does our instruction concentrate so much attention on the breath? We're not doing this to become good breathers or even good meditators. We're doing this to become clear about what is true. So why talk about the breath so much? Breath is a really good point of focus to begin with, even to end with. It's always there. We are all always breathing. If you haven't got any problems with your breathing apparatus, it's a relatively neutral activity to pay attention to. It's uncomplicated, rather plain. For that reason, as we begin to focus on it and pay attention to it, it allows the mind to become somewhat concentrated and calm as well. It's changing all the time, but it's rather steady in its changing. So it's a good tool for focusing and also for calming the attention.

Breathing has the possibility not only of calming and focusing the mind but also of allowing insight to arise. Some people practice throughout their entire lives just by paying attention to breathing. Everything that is true about anything is true about breath: it's impermanent; it arises and it passes away. Yet if you didn't breathe, you would become uncomfortable, so then you would take in a big inhalation and feel comfortable again. But if you hold onto the breath, it's no longer comfortable, so you have to breathe out again. All the time shifting, shifting. Discomfort is continually arising. We see that everything keeps changing. Sometimes people worry that they are not in touch with their breath or cannot find their breath or work with it. Breath takes care of itself. Arising and passing away quite impersonally, with no one breathing. This understanding comes through our attention.

Adapted from "Body as Body," Vol. I, No. 2, Winter 1991

ZEN, OR JUST SITTING

*With Zen meditation, we learn to
sit still with all aspects of ourselves*

by Barry Magid

Imagine sitting down in front of a mirror. Your face automatically appears. There is no effort required; the mirror is doing all the work. You can't do it right or wrong. The Zen Buddhist practice of "just sitting" is like that. When we sit, our mind automatically begins to display itself to us. Our practice is to observe and experience what appears moment after moment. Of course, just as when we look in a real mirror, things don't stay that simple for long.

We notice how our faces or our bodies look in the mirror, and we immediately have an emotional reaction and form judgments about what we see. Rainer Maria Rilke wrote that Paul Cézanne was capable of painting a self-portrait with utter objectivity, of looking at his own face with no more reaction than "a dog which sees itself in a mirror and thinks, 'There is another dog.'" For the rest of us, it's not so easy to simply observe who we are. Looking in the mirror, we are tempted to use it as a makeup mirror to touch up the parts of our self-image we don't like.

Our minds are never what we want them to be. That's part of why we sit in the first place. We are uncomfortable with ourselves as we are. The greatest dualism we face is the split between who we are and who we think we ought to be. Sometimes that gap fuels our aspiration to follow Buddhist teachings, sometimes it simply fuels our self-hatred, and all too often we confuse these two notions of self entirely.

Just sitting means sitting still with all of the aspects of ourselves that we came to Buddhist practice in order to avoid or change—our restlessness, our anxiety, our fear, our anger, our wandering minds. Our practice is to just watch, to just feel. We watch our minds. Minds think. There's no problem with that; minds just do what they do. Ordinarily we get caught up in the content of our thoughts, but when we just sit, we observe ourselves just thinking. Our body's most basic activity is breathing: no matter what else is going on, we are breathing. We sit and breathe, and we feel the sensation of our breath in our bodies. Often there is tension or even pain somewhere in our bodies as well. We sit and feel that too and keep breathing. Whatever thoughts come, come. Whatever feelings come, come. We are not sitting there to fight off our thoughts or try to make ourselves stop thinking.

When we sit, we realize how unwilling we are to leave anything about ourselves alone. We turn our lives into one endless self-improvement project. All too often what we call meditation or spirituality is simply incorporated into our obsession with self-criticism and self-improvement. I've encountered many students who have attempted to use meditation to perform a spiritual lobotomy on themselves—trying to excise, once and for all, their anger, their fear, their sexuality. We have to sit with our resistance to feeling whole, to feeling all those painful and messy parts of ourselves.

Just sitting means just that. That "just" endlessly goes against the grain of our need to fix, transform, and improve ourselves. The paradox of our practice is that the most effective way of transformation is to leave ourselves alone. The more we let everything be just what it is, the more we relax into an open, attentive awareness of one moment after another. Just sitting leaves everything just as it is.

Originally titled "Leave Yourself Alone!" from "Five Practices to Change Your Mind," Vol. XIV, No. 4, Summer 2005

A REFUGE INTO BEING

Q&A with Martine Batchelor

Question: When meditating, is it necessary to focus on one specific object?

This is not always necessary, but at times it can be very helpful. When you do meditate on a specific object, such as the breath, that object will help you to develop concentration, and concentration will enable you to cultivate a quiet and spacious mind. But you must be careful not to focus your attention too narrowly on the object, as that can constrain your practice. You should keep your primary focus on the object of meditation but try to do so with a wide-open awareness. As you follow the breath, for instance, allow yourself to also be aware of what is happening in and around you. Be conscious of sounds, thoughts, sensations, feelings—but without fixating on, grasping, or rejecting any of these things.

When you meditate without a specific object, you are trying to be aware of everything in that moment, without fixation. You simply notice whatever arises— in the world or in the mind—with a nondiscriminatory awareness. This practice of open awareness can help you become restful and spacious; however, you must be careful not to become dreamy. You have to remain alert, still, and present. This requires energy, dedication, and faith in the practice and in your Buddha-nature in that moment.

You must also be careful not to equate meditation solely with concentration. It is essential to cultivate inquiry as well. This is the quality of the mind that sees clearly into the impermanent and conditioned nature of reality. Whether you are focusing on a specific object or not, the cultivation of inquiry requires you to look deeply into and investigate the nature of each phenomenon in your field of awareness. Whether it is the breath or a sound or a thought, each and every thing can be seen as conditioned and constantly changing. It is essential that you cultivate together and in harmony these twin elements of concentration and inquiry. Concentration will bring stability, stillness, and spaciousness; inquiry will bring alertness, vividness, brightness, and clarity. Combined, they will help you to develop creative awareness, an ability to bring a meditative mind to all aspects of your daily life. In this way, meditation becomes both a refuge and a training: a refuge into being and a training in doing.

In the Korean Zen tradition, there is a method of meditation that uses the question "What is this?" to cultivate concentration and inquiry together. As you sit or walk in meditation, you ask constantly, *What is this?* Repeating this question develops concentration because it returns you to the full awareness of the moment. As soon as you become aware of being distracted by past events, anxieties about the present, or future dreams, you ask, *What is this?* This way, the power of questioning dissolves distraction.

You don't repeat this question like a mantra but with a deep sense of questioning. This is not an analytical or intellectual endeavor. (You have to be careful not to ask the question with the head but with the whole body; sometimes it is recommended to ask with the lower belly.) You are not asking about anything specific, and you are not looking for a specific answer. You are just asking meditatively, experientially, opening yourself to the whole moment, to the questionable and mysterious aspect of life itself and your place within it. You are asking because you truly do not know.

As with breath meditation, the question is the primary object of concentration, but it is asked within a wide-open awareness. This kind of meditation helps you to become centered and grounded but open and spacious at the same time. It will enable you to be more flexible and creative by loosening your grasping and fixations. Your heart will open in a wise and compassionate manner to yourself and life in all of its extraordinarily various aspects.

"On the Cushion: A Refuge into Being," Vol. XII, No. 2, Winter 2002

MAY WE ALL
BE HAPPY

*Metta, or lovingkindness meditation,
sends a wish for the well-being
of oneself and others*

by Gil Fronsdal

Metta, or lovingkindness, is one of the most important Buddhist practices. Simply stated, metta is the
heartfelt wish for the well-being of oneself and others.
When describing metta, the Buddha used the analogy
of the care a mother gives her only child. Lovingkindness is also understood as the innate friendliness of an
open heart. Its close connection to friendship is reflected
in its similarity to the Pali word for friend, *mitta*. However, metta is more than conventional friendship, for it
includes being openhearted even toward one's enemies,
developed from insight into our shared humanity.

Metta practice is the cultivation of our capacity for
lovingkindness. It does not involve either positive thinking or the imposition of an artificial positive attitude.
There is no need to feel loving or kind during metta

75

practice. Rather, we meditate on our good intentions, however weak or strong they may be, and water the seeds of these intentions. When we water wholesome intentions instead of expressing unwholesome ones, we develop those wholesome tendencies within us. If these seeds are never watered, they won't grow. When watered by regular practice, they grow, sometimes in unexpected fashions. We may find that lovingkindness becomes the operating motivation in a situation that previously triggered anger or fear.

To practice lovingkindness meditation, sit in a comfortable and relaxed manner. Take two or three deep breaths with slow, long, and complete exhalations. Let go of any concerns or preoccupations. For a few minutes, feel or imagine the breath moving through the center of your chest in the area of your heart.

Metta is first practiced toward oneself, since we often have difficulty loving others without first loving ourselves. Sitting quietly, mentally repeat, slowly and steadily, the following or similar phrases: *May I be happy. May I be well. May I be safe. May I be peaceful and at ease.*

While you say these phrases, allow yourself to sink into the intentions they express. Lovingkindness meditation consists primarily of connecting to the intention of wishing ourselves or others happiness. However, if feelings of warmth, friendliness, or love arise in the body or mind, connect to them, allowing them to grow as you repeat the phrases. As an aid to the meditation, you might hold an image of yourself in your mind's eye. This helps reinforce the intentions expressed in the phrases.

After a period of directing lovingkindness toward yourself, bring to mind a friend or someone in your life who has deeply cared for you. Then slowly repeat phrases of lovingkindness toward him or her: *May you be happy. May you be well. May you be safe. May you be peaceful and at ease.*

As you say these phrases, again sink into their intention or heartfelt meaning. And again, if any feelings of lovingkindness arise, connect the feelings with the phrases so that the feelings may become stronger as you repeat the words.

As you continue the meditation, you can bring to mind other friends, neighbors, acquaintances, strangers, animals, and finally people with whom you have difficulty. You can either use the same phrases, repeating them again and again, or make up phrases that better represent the lovingkindness you feel toward these beings.

Sometimes during lovingkindness meditation, seemingly opposite feelings such as anger, grief, or sadness may arise. Take these to be signs that your heart is softening, revealing what is held there. You can either shift to mindfulness practice or you can—with whatever patience, acceptance, and kindness you can muster for such feelings—direct lovingkindness toward them. Above all, remember that there is no need to judge yourself for having these feelings.

As you become familiar with lovingkindness practice during meditation, you can also begin to use it in your daily life. While in your car or at work or in public, privately practice metta toward those around you. There can be a great delight in establishing a heartfelt connection to everyone we encounter, friends, and strangers alike.

May all beings be happy.
May they live in safety and joy.
All living beings,
Whether weak or strong,
Tall, stout, average, or short,
Seen or unseen, near or distant,
Born or to be born,
May they all be happy.

— From the *Metta Sutta, Sutta Nipata I.8*

"May We All Be Happy," from "Five Practices to Change Your Mind,"
Vol. XIV, No. 4, Summer 2005

GIVING AND TAKING

The basics of tonglen, *a Tibetan Buddhist practice to cultivate compassion*

by Judith Simmer-Brown

Tonglen, literally "giving and taking," is a Tibetan practice for cultivating compassion, the Mahayana path of the bodhisattva. The great master Atisha brought Tibetans this practice from India in the 11th century. Tonglen reverses the pattern of self-cherishing that is the knot of our personal suffering. Using breathing as the basis, tonglen opens our hearts to those things we would rather avoid and encourages us to share those things we would rather keep for ourselves. The practice shows that there are no real boundaries between living beings—we are all interdependent.

We begin tonglen by taking our seats in meditation with good posture, very simply and naturally. We ask, "Why would we want to do this practice?" Fundamentally it is vast and choiceless. We recognize that the purpose of our human life is huge, to grow larger hearts and open minds, and we celebrate that we can do this in this moment. We are ready for transformation. Glimpsing this motivation begins the practice.

Then we become aware of our breathing, in and out, and establish the flow of the practice. On the in-breath, we breathe in thinking *heavy, thick, hot,* and on the out-breath, we breathe out thinking *light, bright, cool.* At first it seems only like words, but it is good to develop a literal sense of this. My teacher, Chögyam Trungpa Rinpoche, suggested that we think of ourselves as air conditioners. We breathe in the stale, smoky, fetid air of the room around us, and we breathe out fresh, clean, cool air. We gradually purify the room. When we breathe, we are breathing with every pore of our bodies, in with *heavy, thick, hot* and out with *light, bright, cool.* Do this for roughly one-third of the 20-minute session, or until the texture is established.

Next, we breathe with a continuing sense of the texture we have established. But now we open our thoughts and emotions to all of our personal material. It is good to start with those who spontaneously arouse our compassion. Is there someone we know who is sick or in emotional turmoil? We begin with that person's face before us and breathe in their heavy, thick, and hot suffering, sharing with them our own light, bright, and cool energy. Be quite tangible with the texture. Whatever suffering we see in them, we breathe it in; whatever sanity and kindness we see in ourselves, we breathe it out to them. When we are ready, extend beyond our loved ones to more difficult people. Are there people we see as threatening or problematic in our lives? We allow their faces to come to us and then breathe in their suffering and extend to them our sanity and kindness. We are practicing embracing what we would normally avoid and sharing what we would normally hoard. Do this part of the practice for 7 to 10 minutes.

We conclude the practice by extending it out beyond our familiar world. One way to do this is to move geographically. We begin in our immediate neighborhood, from the family next door with the two babies, to the college student on the other side who takes terrible care of her lawn, to the elderly woman across the street who recently lost her husband. We move to those people we encounter in our daily routines—our coworkers and our boss; the grocery checker and stock boy; the employees at the cleaners, the gas station, and the video store. Then we extend through our community, to the hospital, the shelter, the jail, the nursing home, including everyone suffering there. And we extend to our state, region, country, and world, our minds going to the painful situations there that are described in the newspaper—the wars, famines, epidemics. We also include the CEOs, the political leaders, and the people of privilege. We extend this practice until the 20-minute session is over. Then we conclude with a simple session of meditation again.

Originally titled "Hot and Heavy, Cool and Light," from "Five Practices to Change Your Mind," Vol. XIV, No. 4, Summer 2005

GUIDED MEDITATION: AWAKENING JOY

by James Baraz

Sit quietly in a relaxed posture. Focus on the heart center (in the middle of your chest.) As you inhale, visualize breathing in benevolent energy from all around you. With each exhalation, allow any negativity to be released.

Reflect on a person or situation in your life you're grateful for. Begin with the phrase "I'm grateful to . . ." or "I'm grateful for . . ."

Invite into your awareness an image of that person or situation. Fully experience your gratitude, taking time to feel in your body the energy of that blessing in your life.

Take a moment to silently send a thought of appreciation to that person or that situation.

Repeat this for 10 minutes, reflecting one by one on the various blessings in your life.

End with the intention to express your gratitude directly to those who've come to mind.

Notice the feeling of well-being as the meditation ends. As an experiment, do this as a daily gratitude practice for a week and notice its effects.

"Awakening Joy: A Guided Meditation," Vol. XIII, No. 4, Summer 2004

WORRY BEADS

*𝓜ala practice brings peace
of body and mind*

by Clark Strand

After nearly 30 years of using and making the prayer beads of various religious traditions, I have come to a simple conclusion: all beads are worry beads—from the Pope's rosary all the way down to those little wrist *malas,* sometimes popularly referred to as "power bracelets," worn by Buddhists and non-Buddhists alike. People of every religious tradition will claim that their beads are for praying—for appealing to a higher power, for collecting the spirit or concentrating mind—and while this is indisputably true, that is not their primary purpose. Beads are for worry. They answer a human need so basic it actually precedes a religious consciousness—and that is to fret over things. The Buddhist mala acknowledges this. It is a way of engaging our worries, a way of combining the universal need for talismanic objects with the kind of repetitive movements that calm the body and mind. The difference between the Buddhist mala and the various Western-style rosaries is simply that it makes this explicit in the symbolism of its beads.

A Buddhist mala typically consists of 108 beads, one for each of the delusions (call them worries) that afflict human life. I am often asked how that number was arrived at, and the answer, although somewhat convoluted mathematically, makes sense from a Buddhist point of view. There are six varieties of delusion that can occur when we experience an object of awareness: delusion via the eyes, the ears, the nose, the tongue, the body, or the mind. Each of these objects can in turn be perceived in the past, the present, or the future, making for 18 possibilities in all. Multiply these by the two conditions of heart (pure and impure) and again by the three possible sentiments with regard to any of those sense objects (like, dislike, and indifference), and the number of possibilities for delusion is found to be 6 x 3 x 2 x 3 . . . or 108. There are other ways of calculating that number, but in most cases the gist is the same. For a Buddhist, delusion is the only legitimate source of worry. Worrying about money or health is, by comparison, relatively pointless. There will never be enough money in the world (that seems to be the point of money), and our health is guaranteed to fail in the end, no matter what we do. The wordless message of the Buddhist mala is "Don't worry about things; worry about the fact that you are so worried all the time, and address the root of that." The mala is a teaching in itself.

At some point in their religious observances, most Mahayana Buddhists recite some variation on the bodhisattva vows, the second of which is "No matter how inexhaustible delusions are, I vow to vanquish them all"—a paradox at best, at worst an impossible task. But the mala offers a valuable clarification on this point, for it is basically a circle. In the course of reciting a round of mantras, one begins and ends with the guru bead. The larger, three-holed bead at the end of a mala is the Buddhist equivalent of the crucifix on a Catholic rosary. It is the teacher—and the teaching—we keep coming back to with every cycle we pray. As a rule we never cross that bead in our counting. Rather, if we want to continue beyond a single cycle, we stop at the guru bead and count the beads back in the opposite direction, repeating this same cycle for as long as we wish to practice. In this way, we find that delusions truly are inexhaustible. Delusion is the realm we live in; delusion is fundamentally what we are. To overcome this, once and for all, is to pass beyond this life. When we have done that, finally, we enter the timeless realm of the Buddha.

What is most peculiar about mala practice is that the beads never take us there. We always stop short of the Buddha realm and turn back the other way. This may seem fatalistic on its surface, but there is a deep wisdom in this simple ritual, for even though he eventually passed into the extinguished, blown-out-candle state of nirvana, the Buddha realized his enlightenment as a human being and lived in peace with all other beings in this world. He is the Tathagata, or the "Thus Come One," not the Thus Gone.

We are not called upon as Buddhists to deny the world and certainly not to escape from it. We are called to live with it and to make our peace with all that is. In Buddhist terms, that peace is called Tathagata. The Thus Come One is as enlightened as he is, not as he would wish himself to be. There is no escaping this. The world of worries we wish to escape from in the beginning of Buddhist practice is found to be enlightenment itself in the end. We don't understand this, of course, and so we keep striving for a distant, idealized kind of Buddha-hood, only to reach its threshold and be turned back the way we came. In this way, we receive the teaching of the Buddha with every mala we say.

That is what the beads have taught me. Now, after many years of handling them, taking in their teachings through the palm of my hand, I am occasionally able to recognize a little of that teaching when I see it manifested in others. There is the Tibetan mother of a friend of mine, dispossessed of her homeland, happily walking through the town where I live, an enormous goiter swelling above the neckline of her traditional dress. She fingers her beads continuously, smiling all the while. She speaks little English, but as I witness her reach the end of her mala and happily twist it about in her hand to finger its beads back the other way, I see that she is at peace in the world, as though she had actually spoken the words aloud: *Buddha. Dharma. Sangha.* The teachings are all there. She carries them. And when she isn't carrying them, she wears them on her sleeve.

PRACTICE: SAYING THE *NEMBUTSU*

Nembutsu literally means "to think of Buddha" and is based on the teaching that "when you are mindful of the Buddha, the Buddha is mindful of you." The principal practice of Pure Land Buddhism, nembutsu originally referred to a complex series of practices leading up to a vision of Amida Buddha in his Western Paradise. But many centuries ago it came to mean just what it does today: simple recitation of the words *Namu Amida Butsu*—"I take refuge in Amida, the Buddha of Infinite Light and Life."

Reciting the nembutsu sets the minds of those who practice it directly in the presence of Amida Buddha, with no intermediary whatsoever. Therefore, it can be taken up by anyone, anywhere, at any time, whether they have received instruction in that practice from a Pure Land teacher or not.

Honen, the founder of the Pure Land school, taught, "The way to say the nembutsu lies in having no way." In other words, any way of saying the nembutsu is fine. You may say it very fast or very slowly, use its traditional six-syllable form, Na-Mu-A-Mi-Da-Bu, or abbreviate it down to Na-Man-Da-Bu, as many Japanese people do; it makes no difference at all. In saying the nembutsu we rely on Amida's Vow to save all beings who simply call upon his name. To be too concerned with such matters as rhythm or pronunciation takes our minds off of the Buddha. And so it is best not to worry. Amida will hear us wherever we are, in whatever condition we find ourselves, and however we say his name.

In reciting the nembutsu, some traditions stress the use of malas, also called *juzu* ("counting beads"), to keep track of their recitations, while others do not. For those who wish to use a juzu, one simply recites the nembutsu once for every bead, turning about at the guru bead to go back in the other direction, repeating this cycle as often as possible. Pure Land practitioners who favor a simple, heartfelt recitation still use malas, only they refer to them as *nenju* ("thought beads"), to indicate that they are not to be used for counting. In such cases, they simply place their hands together in *gassho*, with the beads encircling both palms, and chant.

Placing our hands together in gassho is the basic attitude of devotion in the Pure Land school. The left hand joins the right, palm to palm, and in this way, symbolically speaking, our deluded selves are joined with Amida. When we place our hands together in this way, we find that they match up perfectly. For each finger of the left hand, there is a finger of the right to embrace it. The match is perfect. Nothing is left out.

This is a beautiful description of the way worried beings are saved by Amida. For every moment of delusion, every act of greed, folly, or confusion, there is Amida right beside us, embracing us as we are. If it were necessary to change first in order to be worthy of birth in the Pure Land, few of us could attain it. Fortunately, all that is required is that we unite with the Tathagata. When we join the palms together in this way in an expression of simple faith and utter the words *Namu Amida Butsu,* and whether we count our beads or not, all is taken care of. Amida embraces us on the spot.

Excerpted from "Worry Beads: Meditating with a Mala," Vol. XVI, No. 2, Winter 2006

PART III

MEDITATING
WITH THE
BODY

When we think of Buddhist meditation, we generally think of the mind—and practices that involve attending to our thoughts. We forget that one of the Four Foundations of Mindfulness the Buddha taught is Mindfulness of the Body. (The others are feelings, such as pleasant, unpleasant, or neutral; mind, or consciousness; and mental qualities or objects.)

As the meditation teacher S. N. Goenka points out in "Finding Sense in Sensation," the Buddha discovered that "everything in the mind arises with the sensations on the body and that these sensations are the material we have to work with." Goenka explains the crucial role the body plays in meditation even when we're sitting still on a cushion.

To establish a firm base for meditation, Reginald Ray guides us in an exercise to ground the body ("Earth Breathing"). In "Evolution's Body," Wes Nisker takes us deeper into the body with a series of meditations exploring our evolutionary roots, as well as the body's functioning in whole and in parts. These guided reflections are based on the classic exercises found in the Maha-satipatthana Sutta. Will Johnson offers practices for maintaining awareness of sensations wherever we are ("Full Body, Empty Mind").

Meditating with the body often involves movement. Peter Doobinin introduces us to basic walking meditation ("Awakening, Step by Step"), while Frank Jude Boccio offers instruction in performing yoga asanas—postures—with a meditative mind ("Breath and the Body").

Bowing as a meditative, or contemplative, discipline may seem strange to many Westerners. But as Lama Surya Das explains ("Bowing"), it is a common practice in Asia—a gesture of reverence and respect that centers one in the present moment. As a spiritual exercise, intensive bowing is a way of offering up the self. For Tibetan Buddhists, completing 100,000 prostrations is part of the traditional ngöndro, *or foundational practices for beginning practitioners. For Ch'an and Zen Buddhists, prostrations typically begin and end the meditation period.*

FINDING SENSE IN SENSATION

The crucial role of the body in meditation

by S. N. Goenka

The Buddha was the foremost scientist of mind (*nama*) and matter (*rupa*). What makes him a peerless scientist is his discovery that *tanha*—craving or, by extension, aversion—arises from *vedana*, or sensation on the body.

Before the time of the Buddha, little if any importance was given to bodily sensation. In fact, it was the centrality of bodily sensation that was the Buddha's great discovery in his quest to determine the root cause of suffering and the means to its cessation. Before the Buddha, India's spiritual masters emphasized teachings that encouraged people to turn away from sensory objects and ignore the sensations that contact with them engenders.

But the Buddha, a real scientist, examined sensation more closely. He discovered that when we come into contact with a sense-object through one of the six sense doors (ears, eyes, nose, tongue, body, mind), we cling to the sensation it creates, giving rise to tanha (wanting it to stay and to increase) and aversion (wanting it to cease). The mind then reacts with thoughts of either *I want* or *I do not want*. Buddha discovered that everything that arises in the mind arises with the sensations on the body and that these sensations are the material we have to work with.

The first step, then, is to train the mind to become so sharp and sensitive that it will learn to detect even the subtlest sensations. That job is done by *anapana*—awareness of the breath—on the small area under the nostrils, above the upper lip. If we concentrate on this area, the mind becomes sharper and sharper, subtler and subtler. This is the way we begin to become aware of every sort of sensation on the body.

Next, we feel the sensations but don't react to them. We can learn to maintain this equanimity toward sensations by understanding their transitory nature.

Whether pleasant, unpleasant, or neutral, gross or subtle every sensation shares the same characteristic: it arises and passes away, arises and passes away. It is this arising and passing that we have to experience through practice, not just accept as truth because Buddha said so, not just accept because intellectually it seems logical enough to us. We must experience sensation's nature, understand its flux, and learn not to react to it.

As we reach deeper states of awareness, we will be able to detect subtler and subtler sensations, or vibrations of greater rapidity, arising and passing with greater speed. In these deep states, our mind will become so calm, so tranquil, so pure, that we will immediately recognize any impurity accompanying the agitated state and make the choice to refrain from reacting adversely. It becomes clear to us that we can't harm anybody without first defiling ourselves with emotions like hate or anger or lust. If we do this, we will come to an experiential understanding of the deep truth of *anicca,* or impermanence. As we observe sensations without reacting to them, the impurities in our minds lose their strength and cannot overpower us.

The Buddha was not merely giving sermons; he was offering a technique to help people reach a state in which they could feel the harm they do to themselves. Once we see this, *sila* (ethics) follows naturally. Just as we pull our hand from a flame, we step back from harming ourselves and others.

It is a wonderful discovery that by observing physical sensations on the body, we can eradicate the roots of the defilements of mind. As we practice more, negative emotions will become far more conspicuous to us much earlier; as soon as they arise, we will become aware of sensations and have the opportunity to make ethical choices. But first we need to begin with what is present to us deeply in our minds at the level of sensation. Otherwise, we will keep ourselves and others miserable for a very long time.

"Finding Sense in Sensation," from "The Body: Vehicle for Awakening," Vol. XII, No. 1, Fall 2002

EARTH BREATHING

*A meditation for reconnecting
with the body*

by Reginald Ray

The first step in regaining our embodiment as meditators is to establish a clear, open, and intimate connection with our larger, macrocosmic "body," the earth itself. In this practice, we will explore how the body can be felt as an incarnation of the earth. Earth breathing enables us to deepen our connection with the earth and to explore our identity with the earth itself. This practice also enables us to feel the support the earth offers us. The more we allow ourselves to feel supported by the earth, the more we are able to identify with the earth, the more room we allow ourselves for the inner journey.

Take a good meditation posture and feel the earth under you. Even if you are on a cushion in a room on the sixth floor of a building, you are still supported by the earth. You may initially want to keep your eyes closed. Begin breathing into the perineum, the region between the genital area and the anus. Bring your breath into the bottom of your pelvis at the perineum. Feel any tension you may have in the perineum. Breathe in through your sitting bones. Let the bottom of your pelvis sink into the earth. Breathe into the area of your anal region and your genitals. With each out-breath, let your pelvis sink more and more deeply into the earth, so you are sitting completely and without any reservation on the earth. Bring the energy of the breath up into the hollow of the lower belly.

Now begin to breathe into a point that is a few inches below your perineum, putting you in direct contact with the earth. We are extending our awareness beneath our body, into the earth. Bring the energy of the earth up into your body. Now reach a few inches lower and then a foot lower. You are reaching with your awareness down into the earth and breathing up through your bottom.

With each breath, let your awareness drop down a little further into the earth. Breathe in the inner breath, the inner energy of the earth. Sink lower and lower into the darkness of the earth, breathing the energy up. On the in-breath, you are bringing the energy up, and on the out-breath, you are dropping further down. As you breathe in, allow your attention to remain deep inside the earth.

Continue in this way, letting your mind sink down into the darkness of the earth with each out-breath. Allow yourself to come right to the point where you feel you are about to go to sleep, but stay present and take the attitude that you are sinking into a mysterious realm where all the answers you have ever sought are waiting. Try to be awake yet hovering on the boundary of sleep. On each out-breath let yourself sink a bit deeper, and take note of whatever images arise. Try to sense the extraordinary stillness and peace of the earth.

After about 10 minutes, let your awareness drop more precipitously, further into the earth: 100 feet, 200 feet, a mile. See how far you can reach. Continue to breathe the earth's energy up into your lower belly, going further down each time. Then let the bottom drop out and let your awareness go in a downward freefall. As your awareness descends, gradually have the sense that the energy is filling your body: into your belly, your mid-chest, your upper chest, and your head. Keep reaching down, deeper and deeper. Continue reaching further and further, while continuing to let the energy further up into your body. We are now receiving the awakened energy of the earth in our entire body.

To conclude this practice session, transition by dropping all techniques. Simply sit in your body, feeling your body as a mountain, still and immovable, and notice the awake and present quality of your mind.

Originally titled "Digging Deep," from "Touching Enlightenment," Vol. XV, No. 3, Spring 2006

Evolution's Body

*Guided reflections for experiencing
the body in depth*

by Wes Nisker

In the *Samyutta Nikaya*, the Buddha says, "This body is not mine or anyone else's. It has arisen due to past causes and conditions." The Buddha intuited some type of evolutionary process that creates our bodies, and his essential point is that they are neither formed nor owned by us. We now have evidence that our bodies arise from the forces and elements that make up the entire universe, through a complex chain of interdependent events. Internalizing this understanding can help liberate us from the powerful sense of ownership and attachment we have to the body, which is a cause of tremendous suffering, especially as the body grows old and we must face its inevitable destiny.

The following guided reflections from the Buddha are adapted from the classic exercises on mindfulness of body found in the *Maha-satipatthana Sutta*. Here we combine the experiential aspect of bringing mindfulness to various parts of the body with some simple reflection on the evolutionary origin of those body parts. These exercises can help to reveal that this body is not ours; it is evolution's body. The body we live in is a loaner. The exercises are best done in a seated position (sitting in a chair is fine), keeping the spine as straight as possible. It is useful to read through the entire series of exercises and then return to the beginning and focus on a single reflection at a time. After reading a reflection on one particular body part or function, close your eyes and bring your attention to that area of the body and begin the exercise. These reflections can be done in any order or separately, and you may take as long as you wish for any of them.

THE BODY AND THE ELEMENTS

Begin by bringing attention to your entire body, and for a few moments just feel the body's warmth and strength, its ability to hold itself upright. The vitality and aliveness that you experience in your body require various chemical and mineral substances, a continuous supply of oxygen, the energy of the sun, and the cohesion and conductivity of water. The Buddha instructs us to reflect on the body as composed of the elements of earth, air, fire, and water, so that we will see how this life is interwoven with universal processes.

Resting attention on your breath for a few moments, sense the fact that you are located in an atmosphere— the medium through which you move and by which your body lives. Can you feel the air all around you as a substance? Move your arm and feel it parting the air, almost as if you were swimming through this medium.

Now bring attention to your breathing, and simultaneously look at a plant in your house or the plants growing outside, and realize that with each breath you are feeding the plants and being fed by them. Doing this simple reflection just a few times can begin to alter your feelings about the plant kingdom.

As you sense yourself exchanging nutrients with the plants, you will be able to recognize that you are not only located in an atmosphere but an integral part of it. With every breath you are participating in the great cycles of water and gases, the hydrosphere and atmosphere. With each breath you are joining in the single great breath of all earth life.

THE SKELETAL FRAME

Focus attention on the great bone of your skull. Let awareness roam over the entire area of your head, feeling this massive bone that houses the delicate brain. Notice the holes conveniently placed for the sense organs of hearing, smelling, tasting, and seeing, and the great opening at the bottom of the skull for the spine to enter. It has taken 500 million years of vertebrate evolution to get your skull into this shape, with its narrow, brooding forehead.

To get a better sense of the skull bone, gently clench your jaw and grind your teeth together a little. As you feel the power of your jaw, you might reflect on the fact that the jaw began developing in an early, wormlike marine creature, which gained great survival advantage with the newfound ability to eat things that were bigger than itself. The vast number of chewers now alive in the world testifies to the usefulness of this powerful hinge.

Next, move awareness down from the skull into your spine and ribs. See if you can sense the entire skeleton of bones extending outward from that central ridgepole of spine. If you move your limbs or head around a little, you might get a kinesthetic sense of the skeletal structure. You could also visualize the skeletons you have seen from Halloween, anatomy books, or Grateful Dead posters. As you visualize and feel the bone structure, be aware that there are more than 600 separate bones in your body.

While you are feeling the entire skeleton, you might also reflect for a moment on the fact that our bones are composed of calcium phosphate. They are, quite literally, the clay of earth, molded into our human shape. Our bodies are not only on the earth, they are of the earth. When seated or walking, you can feel your body as a kind of earth sprout that gained mobility.

While on the subject of bones, we can draw a good lesson in dharma practice from the early microbes, which apparently were irritated by calcium phosphate and other sea salts and would flush them from their bodies. Then some enterprising microbes, perhaps after "sitting through" the irritation (so to speak), discovered that the mineral substances could help protect their bodies. Thus the bones of the first skeleton began to take shape. It is interesting to note that in mineral content and porosity, human bones are nearly identical to certain species of South Pacific coral, and plastic surgeons have begun to use this coral to fix and replace human bone.

THE DIGESTIVE SYSTEM

Next, move your mindful awareness to your stomach area. Although you may not feel many distinct sensations, let your awareness linger there as you reflect on some of the activity taking place in this region of your body. For instance, at this moment, along with digestion taking place—nutrients being extracted from food substances and waste being processed for disposal—there are thousands of cells being born and dying. Your stomach contains hundreds of thousands of digestive glands, and the stomach must produce a new lining every three days to protect itself from its own digestive juices. For this task, your stomach is producing up to 500,000 new cells every minute.

Along with all of this activity, you might consider that at this very moment there are more living beings inside your stomach than all the humans who have ever lived on earth. Considering the billions of bacteria and microbes that live inside each of us, microbiologist Lynn Margulis writes, "Our concept of the individual is totally warped. All of us are walking communities." We are not separate selves. Each of us is an ecosystem.

THE HANDS

Bring attention to your hands. Spread your fingers out, wiggle them, press them against your palm and thumb. The five-digit design of your hands goes back 370 million years to the first land vertebrates, called tetrapods. Maybe five digits were the minimum number needed to hold on to the land and not slip back into the sea. As you feel your hands, consider that just two million years ago, a blink in biological time, our ancestors could barely manipulate rocks and sticks, and now some of our hands can play the piano, type over 100 words a minute, and build rockets and computers. You can experience the great dexterity of your hands right now, by simply unbuttoning a button. You don't even consciously have to direct those movements! Our hands (and brains) definitely deserve a round of applause.

As you clap, you might also notice the flexibility of your wrists. Most people can move their wrists around in an arc of almost 360 degrees, and our shoulders are almost as flexible. According to the evolutionary biologists, this range of movement in our wrists and shoulders came about because for millions of years our ancestors got around by swinging through the trees. How many of our physical characteristics are inherited from the life that came before?

Recent research indicates that the dexterity of our hands was also very important in the growth of our brains. As our hands began to manipulate tools, a bigger brain was required to direct the movements and store the enormous new amounts of information being learned. The interaction and mutual stimulation of hand and brain created an evolutionary feedback loop in which both developed to an unprecedented degree. As you move your fingers around—buttoning, typing, playing an instrument—you might reflect on the complex activity going on simultaneously in your brain to direct those movements.

As we feel our arms and hands, we can also reflect that these appendages were once fins, and not just in our distant ancestors. Each of us, in the womb, develops both fin- and gill-like structures as we cycle through the genetic instructions of the many life forms that preceded us. Our body and brain are built out of the triumphs and defeats of all earth life, an amazingly complex stream of causes and conditions.

THE WHOLE BODY

Finally, bring awareness to your entire body, sensing the complete organism. Feel the energies within the body, the streams of sensation, the points of twitching or tension, the great pulses of breath and heartbeat.

Realize how much activity is taking place at this moment within you—and without you. Right now there are literally millions of brain cells firing signals to one another, a veritable storm of electrical activity taking place inside your head. Your brain stem is busy monitoring your body temperature and rate of heartbeat, while your limbic system remains on alert for possible survival threats and opportunities.

Meanwhile, oxygen is being inhaled and transported throughout your body and burned as fuel in the process of transforming the stored energy of the sun into your own living energy. In every second, millions of cells are dying and millions more are being created. Chemicals that do the work of the brain, stomach, liver, and kidneys are being manufactured and secreted. As we contemplate our body, we begin to realize that we don't direct most of these processes. We don't live, so much as life lives through us.

These are just a few reflections on the evolutionary sources of the body and behaviors: they are practices of both deep ecology and self-liberation. Using scientific information as a skillful means, we can experience what has been called our "ecological self," or "species self." Through such exercises we can begin to realize that our individual human life is first and foremost life; second, it is human; and only third is it individual. Getting to know ourselves as biological beings, interwoven with all of earth's elements and other forms of life, can be a good source of both our liberation and our compassion.

"Evolution's Body," Vol. X, No. 1, Fall 2000

FULL BODY, EMPTY MIND

Physical sensations as a doorway to personal growth and spiritual transformation

by Will Johnson

As the 11th-century Mahamudra teacher Tilopa said, "Do nothing with the body but relax." When we start to relax, we start feeling the body. Tensions and contractions in the body serve as a numbing blanket that keeps the tiny physical sensations that exist on every part of the body from being felt. Learning how to relax while remaining upright in the sitting posture allows the body's full range of sensations to come out of hiding and make their existence felt. It's always struck me as peculiar. *If I know that sensations can be felt to exist everywhere in the body, then why don't I feel them? And what effect does blocking out awareness of feeling have on me? And finally, if the mind that is "lost in thought" is somehow dependent on my not feeling the sensations of the body, what happens to the mind if I let myself feel the entire body, head to toe, as an unbroken field of sensations?* The sitting posture itself can be a kind of crucible for burning off the tensions and restrictions to body and breath that all too often keep us lost in thought and unaware of feeling presence.

A good place to start is examining what happens to the body when you're lost in thought. This, of course, is tricky to do because when the mind is off wandering in involuntary thought, you're not very aware of the body at all. But if you can include an observation of the body while you're off in a thought, you'll find that the condition "lost in thought" is directly accompanied somewhere in the body by muscular contraction and tensing, stillness and rigidity, and a subtle contraction or holding quality to the breath. In other words, when you're lost in thought, you're tense in body. It follows, then, that if you can consciously work with the body during your sitting practice, to soften and relax the tensions and allow more resilient and natural movement to accompany the passage of the breath, the chatter of the mind can be reduced, and your practice can start going really deep.

As important as formal practices undeniably are, I feel that it is even more important to view the rest of our lives as informal practice. What I mean by this is that the awareness of embodied presence need not be confined to the time spent sitting on our meditation cushion. Every single moment provides an opportunity to relax the tendency to create tension in the body and unconscious thought patterns in the mind, and this can be a very gentle process. If intensive retreats are like turning up the flame on the stove, informal practice is like simmering at a low and steady heat that is practically unnoticeable and so allows you to go about your daily life without the emotional upheavals that can occur during more intensive periods of practice.

I think of informal practice as embodied mindfulness. In truth, every single moment of our lives presents us with a choice: either awaken to the reality of the present moment or stay sleepy and push aspects of that reality away. Sensations are here every single moment. Why don't we feel them? The visual field, in all its dazzling play, is here every moment that our eyes are open. Can we remember to look and actually see? Sounds are here constantly. Blocking them from our awareness creates a great deal of tension in the body.

Let alignment, relaxation, and surrendered resilience be your physical guides not only in your sitting practice but also as you go about your day. These three keys allow you to stay in touch with embodied presence. Merging an awareness of body with the awareness of vision and sound allows you to truly become one with this present moment. As you bring alignment, relaxation, and resilience into your daily life, your breath automatically becomes fuller and starts moving through your entire body, just as the Buddha suggested in his description of meditation. Without forcing a thing, let your breath breathe you: breathe into your entire body, and breathe out just as effortlessly. This condition, nothing more, nothing less, is really the reward and benefit of the practice. And in this way you can walk in full awareness through the city or countryside, like a knife cutting through the softest butter. Always be on the lookout not to bring any tension into this practice. Striving to attain this kind of awareness is simply self-defeating. Relax into presence. It's been there all the time.

EXERCISE: DISSOLVING THOUGHT
INTO SENSATION

Sensation and thought cannot easily coexist. Another way of saying this is that sensation and thought cannot occupy the same space. So, locate where your next thought is positioned in space. It's probably going to be somewhere around or inside your head, but it's definitely somewhere in your body. Find out where it is. Plot out its spatial coordinates. Where does it start and stop in your body? What shape is it?

Now shift your awareness. Remember: sensations exist in every part of the body, and thought and sensation cannot occupy the same space. So, relax and let yourself start to feel the tactile sensations, the feeling presence, that also occupies that space. Just let the feeling presence in this space start to come forward. Where is your thought now?

EXERCISE: EXPANDING SENSATION
INTO PRESENCE

Never look upon the involuntary thought process of the mind as an enemy that needs to be subdued or vanquished. Look upon it instead as an infallible guide that is constantly "re-minding" you that you have momentarily lost awareness of sensations. Once you have dissolved thought into sensation in the area of your head, expand your awareness of sensations to include your entire body. Without bringing any tension into this shifting of awareness, staying completely relaxed, feel the entire body from head to foot, all at once, as a unified field of tactile sensations.

Now expand your awareness to include the entire field of vision. Soften any tension around your eyes so that you can see the entire visual field all at once. Next include the entire field of sound. Be aware of every little bit of the ever-changing field of sound, as though you were listening to a symphony and hearing what every single instrument was playing.

Feel the entire body. See the entire visual field. Listen to everything that is here to be heard. Stay completely relaxed as you do this. In this condition of awakened presence, where have the thoughts gone? Where have *you* gone?

Excerpted from "Full Body, Empty Mind," an interview by Andrew Merz, Vol. XVII, No. 1, Fall 2007

AWAKENING,
STEP BY STEP

An introduction to walking meditation

by Peter Doobinin

Walking meditation is a practice through which we develop concentration and mindfulness. We learn to cultivate mindfulness of the body while the body is moving. We learn to be awake. Walking meditation is a particularly important practice in that it enables us to make the transition from sitting meditation to being awake in our daily lives, in our work, and in our relationships. In the end, that's what it's all about.

Walking meditation is a simple practice. You choose a straight path—indoors or outdoors—roughly 15 or 20 steps long. You walk from one end of the path to the other, turn around, and walk back. You continue in this fashion, walking back and forth, focusing your attention on your feet. Your posture is upright, alert, and relaxed. You can hold your hands at your sides or clasped in front or behind. Keep your eyes open, cast down, and slightly ahead. You can experiment with your pace, perhaps walking quite slowly or at a more regular speed, in an effort to find the pace at which you're most present. As you walk, direct your attention to the sensations in the feet, to the bare experience of walking. Try to feel one step at a time. Be fully, wholeheartedly aware of the physical sensations involved in taking each step. Feel your foot as it lifts, moves through the air, makes contact with the ground. In particular, pay attention to the touching down of the foot, the sensations of contact and pressure. Remember that you're feeling each step, you're not thinking about the foot or visualizing it.

You'll find, of course, that it isn't always easy to stay focused on the meditation object, the sensations in the feet. The mind wanders, drifts. Your job is to notice when you've strayed, when you're lost in thought. Be aware that you've wandered. And return gently to the physical sensations, the lifting, moving, placing of the foot. Just keep bringing your attention back.

As you walk, cultivate a sense of ease. There's no hurry to get anywhere, no destination to reach. You're just walking. This is a good instruction: just walk.

As you walk, as you let go of the desire to get somewhere, you begin to sense the joy in simply walking, in being in the present moment. You begin to comprehend the preciousness of each step. It's an extraordinarily precious experience to walk on this earth.

You can start by practicing walking meditation for 10 minutes a day. Gradually, you can expand the amount of time you spend on this formal walking meditation.

In addition to this kind of formal practice, you'll want to practice walking meditation in "real life" situations. You can practice informally just about anywhere—walking along a city sidewalk, down the aisle in the supermarket, or across the backyard. As always, the objective is to pay attention. Pay attention to your feet. Or pay attention to your whole body—the felt experience of your body as it's moving. In this informal context, you're aware, to some extent, of what's going on around you, but your focus is on your walking. Practicing in this way, you begin to live more mindfully. This is when meditation practice takes hold and assumes a new relevancy. Being awake is no longer reserved for the times you spend in formal sitting meditation; it is the way you live.

"Awakening, Step by Step," from "Five Practices to Change Your Mind," Vol. XIV, No. 4, Summer 2005

BREATH AND
THE BODY

*Seven yoga postures to invigorate
the meditative mind*

by Frank Jude Boccio

Over the past three decades, many Buddhist meditators have been drawn to hatha yoga for the ease and strength it can bring to the body, while many yoga students have turned to Buddhist meditation for the deepening of awareness, insight, and equanimity it can cultivate.

While this complementary approach has much to offer, I have found that a deeper, more integrated, comprehensive approach is possible—and may even be necessary—if one truly wishes to practice yoga holistically. The complementary approach still looks at yoga and Buddhism as different, with the difference being that yoga is understood to be about the body, and Buddhism (and meditation in general) about the mind. A deeper investigation of just what is happening when we practice will quickly reveal the inaccuracy of such a view. When we sit in meditation, much of the work is related to how we experience the body and how we react to that experience. And when we are practicing the *asanas* (postures) of hatha yoga, our minds tend to constantly run commentary, react with story lines and judgments, wander from what we are doing, lean toward the future and away from the past, grasp the pleasant, and push away the unpleasant—just exactly what they do when we sit in meditation.

The Sanskrit word yoga, meaning "union," derives from a verbal root, *yuj,* "to yoke"—what we do when we restrain our attention from wandering as we sit in meditation. From the very beginning, the prime activity of the yogi was to sit in meditation. The posture one takes in sitting meditation is the fundamental asana and is described by the sage Patanjali (second century C.E.) in his Yoga Sutra—the foundational text of classical yoga—as that posture which is both stable and easeful.

While the asanas of hatha yoga are what most Westerners are familiar with as yoga, the truth is that such postures were developed rather late in the history of the yogic tradition. For most of yoga's history, meditation, chanting, selfless service, and study were the main practices of yogis and yoginis.

The word yoga as "union" refers to the integration of body, breath, and mind and to the dissolution of the sense of separation between the "self" as subject of experience and the "other" as object of experience. Whenever this state of embodied integration manifests—whether one is sitting, walking, cutting carrots, or changing diapers—there is yoga.

The Buddha's teaching of the Four Noble Truths and the Eightfold Path is a model of yogic theory and practice. While the Buddha taught a variety of methods of practice, mindfulness is an essential aspect shared by them all. The Sanskrit word *smriti,* most often translated in Buddhist contexts as "mindfulness" or "awareness," literally means "what has been remembered." To "remember" is to "re-collect," to bring back together all the seemingly disparate aspects of our experience into an integrated whole. In this way, remembering is synonymous with the definition of yoga itself. Whenever we see that our minds have wandered from the intimate, immediate, spontaneous, and obvious experience at hand, we remember to come back—to just this, right here and now, using the breath as the yoke.

In the *Bhaddekaratta Sutta,* the Buddha taught, "Looking deeply at life as it is in the very here and now, the practitioner dwells in stability and freedom"—a teaching that echoes Patanjali's definition of asana as "stable and easeful." In both the *Anapanasati Sutta* (Awareness of Breathing) and the *Satipatthana Sutta* (Foundations of Mindfulness), the Buddha tells us to observe the breath and then extend our awareness out to include the whole body. He says that the practitioner should be aware of the movements and positions of the body, "bending down, or standing, walking, sitting, or lying down."

The applicability of this teaching to asana practice is obvious. When we combine awareness of breathing with asana practice, we can look to see how movement affects the breath and how the breath moves the body. We can become aware of habitual patterns of reactivity. For instance, do you hold your breath when you reach out with your arms into a deep stretch? Do you unnecessarily tense muscles not involved with the movement you are making? Do you compare one side of the body with the other when doing asymmetrical postures?

When you repeat a movement, do you find your mind wandering in boredom? As you maintain a posture, can you observe the constantly changing phenomena, or do you solidify the experience, conceptualizing and then relating to the phenomena as a "thing," and either resist or grasp at it, depending on whether you find it pleasant or unpleasant?

Continuing to look deeply, we can begin to see our conditioned aversion to and grasping at different aspects of our experience. The Four Foundations of Mindfulness taught by the Buddha include body, feelings (sensations), mental formations (mind), and phenomena that arise as objects of mind. When practicing asana, we can devote our practice to any one of these, or work through them sequentially.

In the following short sequence, I have chosen several asanas that provide an example of how we can approach the practice of asana as a vehicle of mindfulness and insight. They also function as postures and stretches that can strengthen our capacity for sitting meditation. As you move through them, please go slowly; explore with an investigative, nonjudgmental mind, just as you would in sitting practice. Honor your body's present limitations, while letting go of any mental reactivity that may arise.

CORPSE POSE

Lie on your back with your feet between 12 and 18 inches apart, arms at your sides a few inches away from the torso with the palms up. Surrender the full weight of the body to gravity. Let the earth fully support the body.

This is one of the four major meditation postures taught by the Buddha.

Spend some time resting your awareness on your breath, wherever it is that you feel it in the body. Letting go of any tendency to manipulate it, simply know an in-breath as an in-breath, an out-breath as an out-breath. Working with the First Foundation, open to the breath and its various qualities: deep or shallow, fast or slow, rough or smooth, even or uneven. Scan the body. Is it fully released or still holding tension? When the mind wanders, gently—free of irritation and judgment—bring it back to the breath and the body.

RECLINING PIGEON

From Corpse, bend your knees and bring both feet toward you, near the buttocks, hip width apart. Cross your right leg over your left, placing the outer right shin (just above the ankle) on your left thigh. Then, bringing your left knee into your chest, reach between your legs with your right arm and around the outside of your left leg with your left arm and clasp your hands either just below your left knee or behind the knee on the back of your left thigh. Notice if you held or restricted your breath as you moved into this stretch, and continue to let the breath flow naturally.

Depending on the degree of openness in your hips, you may feel stretching sensations in your right hip. You may also sense some resistance to the sensations manifesting as tensing of the surrounding muscles. See if you can release this tension, and observe how the sensations change as you maintain the stretch. Begin to establish mindfulness of the body (the breath, the body's movements and position); feelings (sensations that you may be experiencing as pleasant or unpleasant); mental formations (the resistance and aversion behind the muscle tensing); and objects of mind. Keep in mind that all phenomena are objects of mind: this means that we can focus our mindfulness not just on the body, sensations, and mental formations but also on the impermanent, non-self nature of these sensations and mental formations; this focus will lead to—perhaps—the cessation of the clinging identification with the experience, the letting go of aversion, and a state of equanimity.

When you do the stretch to the right side, be aware of any subtle, or not so subtle, comparing and judging in the mind. Since we are not perfectly symmetrical beings, you may find that one hip provokes stronger sensations and reactivity than the other. One of my students once remarked that her left side was "the evil twin" of the right. It is just this setting apart in the mind that we try to avoid. Can we stay with the bare sensation, maybe even see the difference from one side to the other, without getting caught in judging or picking and choosing?

CAT/COW

Coming onto your hands and knees, position your hands under your shoulders and your knees under your hips. As you exhale, round your back, pressing your spine up toward the ceiling, tilting the pelvis backward, scooping the tailbone between your legs. Let the head tilt forward so you are gazing back toward your thighs. On the inhalation, tilt the pelvis forward, opening your belly toward the floor and letting your spine move into the torso, creating a gentle backbend. Both the crown of your head and your tailbone reach up toward the ceiling. Be careful not to reach upward with your chin, which compresses the back of the neck.

As you continue to coordinate the movement with your breath, let the duration of the breath determine your pace. Notice how once you have gone back and forth several times, the natural tendency of the mind is to wander. This is our common reaction to repetition. It is as if our mind assumes that having done it already, it knows all about it and needn't pay attention. This "knowing mind" is often the biggest obstacle to intimacy, whether with the experiences of our life or with others. Thinking we know, we stop listening and seeing. Keep the "don't-know mind" and grow in understanding and intimacy. Keep remembering to come back to the breath, the very thread that keeps body and mind connected.

DOWNWARD-FACING DOG

From Cat/Cow, tuck your toes under and, reaching up and back with your sitting bones, straighten your legs into Downward-Facing Dog. You may wish to keep your knees slightly bent at first and emphasize extending your back. Playfully explore the pose, stretching out the right calf by reaching the right heel to the floor, feeling the sensations as you linger here, breathing, and then alternate and stretch out the left leg. If you decide to alternate back and forth, coordinate with the breath and note the tendency of the mind to wander in the face of repetition.

Once you choose to straighten both legs, stay in the posture for anywhere from 8 to 15 breaths, staying alert to sensations, any mental formations that arise, as well as how the experience continuously changes. We tend to speak about "holding" the postures, but notice how there actually is no fixed thing to hold onto. Moment by moment, breath by breath, the posture is continuously re-created. The Dog of the first breath is not the same as the Dog of the sixth breath.

With practice, we begin to see that this is true not only for this asana—and all the other asanas—but also for all our experiences. We come to see that we are not the same person when we come out of the posture that we were when we went into it.

MOUNTAIN

Another of the meditation postures singled out by the Buddha, Mountain is too often perceived as just something we do between the more important asanas, while in fact it is foundational for all the standing postures. Pressing the four corners of your feet (the ball of your big toe, the point directly below your inner ankle, the ball of your little toe, and the point directly below your outer ankle) into the ground, distribute the weight of your body evenly between both feet and centered just in front of your heels. Imagine the pelvis as a bowl with its rim level front to back and side to side. Let the spine rise up, keep the lower ribs from jutting out, gently lift the chest, and open the heart. Relax the shoulders, with your shoulder blades moving into and supporting your upper back. Keep the chin parallel with the floor, not tilted up or down, but gently drawn in so that your ears are centered over your shoulders.

See what happens as you simply stand there. Be awake to all the sensations that arise, the subtle swaying of the body, the movement of the breath. Is there boredom, impatience, or anticipation arising? Can you just be here? When you feel you've been here long enough, take another six to eight breaths and see what happens.

WARRIOR TWO

Reach out to the sides with your arms parallel to the floor and step your feet apart so that they are directly under your fingertips. Turn your left foot in about 15 degrees and your right foot out 90 degrees. Without leaning forward, just bend the right knee toward a 90-degree angle so that the knee is directly over the ankle. Keeping your arms parallel to the ground, gaze out over your right hand.

As you breathe, stay alert to changes in the quality of the breath, its depth and rate. As sensations begin to arise in your front thigh or in your shoulders, notice how the mind reacts with aversion, creating a "psychic amputation" as you tense around the sensations. See what happens to the quality of your experience if you stay with the breath while releasing this aversive tension. Notice the story lines that arise about what is happening and choose to just listen without grasping at any of them. Rather than solidifying the sensations into entities with which to do battle, embrace them with awareness. Notice, if you can, their conditioned, nonpersonal nature. With the letting go of aversion and self-identification, is there a qualitative difference in the experience? As one student put it, "There is a difference between discomfort and suffering." The letting go of the mental anguish that we add to an experience is what the Buddha referred to as *ceto-vimutti*, "release of the mind," a term often used in the Pali canon to signify enlightenment.

After doing this posture on both right and left sides, come back to Mountain and just scan through the body, open to all that arises.

SEATED FORWARD BEND

Sitting with your legs straight out in front of you, press the backs of your thighs, calves, and heels evenly into the ground while reaching through your heels and flexing your toes toward your head. Press your hands into the ground beside your hips as you lift the chest. Think of this as Mountain with a 90-degree bend in it. If your lower back rounds and your weight is coming onto your tailbone, sit on a blanket or two to raise you onto your sitting bones and allow the back to maintain its natural curvature. Grasp your feet or your shins, soften your groin and slightly rotate your thighs inward. Rather than trying to pull your torso onto your legs, lift your torso out over your legs, keeping the lower back from rounding. Those with tight hamstrings will feel this without having to bend forward very far. Let go of "grasping mind" and be where you are. Eventually, those who are more flexible will be able to draw the chest out onto the thighs, and the chin will come to rest on the shins.

Seated forward bends help cultivate a turning within and often come toward the end of an asana session. Feel the breath move within the body. Let go of any physical or mental tension. Surrender into the posture, and keep letting go of any clinging or aversion to the ever-changing phenomena. Notice how the attempt to prolong or create pleasant feelings is itself a form of tension, as is the act of resisting and pushing. Cultivate equanimity and compassion by staying open to all that arises.

When you are ready to come out of the pose, rest on your back, holding both knees into your chest. You may wish to take a gentle reclined spinal twist by letting the knees drop first toward one side of the body for a minute or so and then toward the other side. When ready, rest in Corpse for a few minutes, letting the experience of the practice penetrate the body-mind. While asana practiced this way is indeed a form of meditation in action, sitting after asana practice is often a much more nourishing and satisfying endeavor. Why not try it now?

Excerpted from "Breath and the Body," Vol. XV, No. 1, Fall 2005

BOWING

*An ancient practice centers
us in the present moment*

by Lama Surya Das

Bowing is a common practice in Asia, both within and outside religious circles, a way of expressing respect and reverence, as well as a form of greeting. Tibetans bow and say *"Tashi delek,"* meaning "excellent luck and auspicious good fortune to you." Disciples and devotees bow to their teachers, to the gods, and to holy icons. Buddhists commonly offer bows when entering or leaving a temple, shrine, pilgrimage site, or spiritual circle of any kind, as well as when entering the presence of spiritual masters and teachers, acknowledging the presence of an embodiment of the principle of enlightenment. Zen Buddhists use a short form of the bow, simply placing their palms together at the heart and inclining the torso; this is called *gassho* in Japanese.

Bringing the two hands together at the heart represents the reunion of all polarities and duality in our spiritual center, the heart of enlightenment. Bowing is a way of being, a way of giving, of offering up and opening oneself. Bowing

126

helps us to be centered in the present moment and become more uncomplicated, vulnerable, and humble.

The 7th-century Indian Buddhist master Shantideva said that just to raise one's hand in a gesture of respect and reverence sows the seed of enlightenment. Since his time, bowing has become an intensive spiritual exercise for Buddhists. The devout get down on their hands and knees and then lower themselves face down and flat on the floor; this is a full bow, called a prostration. This gesture symbolizes yielding, surrender, reverence, and taking refuge in that which is good, true, and holy. In fact, this outer form of reverence simply reflects an inner gesture of awareness.

Prostrations such as these are an important part of the most common foundational practices of Tibetan Buddhism, called *ngöndro*, or preliminary practices. Over the course of several months or more, the beginning practitioner is expected to complete over 100,000 of these full-body prostrations, along with chanted Refuge Prayers. It is also something Tibetan Buddhists continue to practice, in fewer repetitions on a daily basis, throughout their lives. The late Tibetan master Kalu Rinpoche explained that prostrating our five limbs (arms, legs, head) on the ground reintegrates our separate sense of being into oneness with the original nature of the five elements.

Buddhist scripture tells us that the Buddha realized his great awakening while sitting beneath a tree in the wilderness of northern India at Bodh Gaya. According to the sutras, when he awoke on that auspicious day, the entire natural world bowed to him in gladness, recognition, and veneration. We join in reverence and enter into that moment each time we bow.

Introduction to "Bowing: A Portfolio by Steve McCurry," Vol. XIII, No. 3, Spring 2004

PART IV

EVERYDAY
PRACTICE

Meditation isn't just a technique to use when sitting on a cushion or walking mindfully or practicing yoga. Mindfulness and compassion are skills we can develop wherever we are and whatever we're doing.

In a sense, everyday meditation is the most powerful practice of all. Unless we can learn to live with equanimity amid the chaos of modern life, all the hours spent on the meditation cushion are unlikely to bring us inner peace and freedom. And the insights and steadiness we gain from right action off the cushion will help to deepen our practice when we sit.

So what does practicing in daily life involve? One of the most important practices is dana, or generosity: it opens our hearts to others, as Marcia Rose reveals in "Cultivating Generosity."

Making sure what we say is right speech—speech that is truthful and causes no harm—is another critical practice to engage in throughout the day. In fact, right speech is so essential for ending suffering that it is one of the steps on the Buddha's Eightfold Path to awakening. In "Giving Up Gossip," Bhikshuni Thubten Chodron suggests ways to check unskillful speech and infuse our words with kindness.

The workplace is an excellent forum for practice. In "Challenges at Work," Michael Carroll draws on a traditional Tibetan Buddhist teaching for handling conflict. Mealtime is another potential minefield we face every day. Anyone having trouble sticking to a diet or eating healthy might benefit from the practices Sandra Weinberg sets out in "Just Say No."

Accepting "what is" is essential for living a balanced life. In "Finding Patience," Michele McDonald offers suggestions on developing patience in the face of day-to-day stresses and frustrating situations.

As a contemplative practice, connecting with nature can be effective in calming and steadying the mind. Mark Coleman, who leads wilderness meditation retreats, sets out seven different exercises in "A Breath of Fresh Air."

In his teachings, the Burmese master Sayadaw U Tejaniya emphasizes the practice of mindfulness in daily life. In a conversation with Tricycle *editor James Shaheen, he describes techniques that helped him overcome depression and cultivate awareness ("The Wise Investigator").*

Anicca, or impermanence, is a central teaching of the Buddha—one of the three fundamental characteristics of existence, along with anatta *(non-self) and* dukkha *(suffering). In "Practicing with Loss," Lama Surya Das offers a meditation on the nature of impermanence, along with an exercise for learning from the inevitable losses life brings.*

CULTIVATING GENEROSITY

Practices to transform greed and self-centeredness

by Marcia Rose

The Buddha said, "If you knew as I know the benefit of generosity, you would not let an opportunity go by without sharing." The Buddha taught and lived what is really a way of life: giving and receiving—the practice of *dana*. The cultivation of dana offers the possibility of purifying and transforming greed, clinging, and self-centeredness, as well as the fear that is linked to these energies of attachment. Dana practice is the foundation of Buddhist spiritual development. Generosity is the ground of compassion; it is a prerequisite for the realization of liberation.

The Tibetans have a practice to cultivate generosity. They take an ordinary everyday object such as a potato or a turnip and hold it in one hand, then pass it to the other hand, back and forth, until it becomes easy. They then move on to objects of seemingly greater value, such as a mound of precious jewels or rice. This "giving" from hand to hand ultimately becomes a symbolic relinquishment of everything—our outer material attachments and our inner attachments, our habits, preferences, ideas, and beliefs—a symbolic letting go of all the ways that we create a "self" over and over again. In our Vipassana practice, this is really what we are doing, but without the props. We learn to give and to receive, letting go of control, receiving what is given—receiving each moment of our lives just as it is, with the trust that it is just right, just enough for our spiritual growth to unfold from.

As our dana practice deepens, we begin to know more directly the ephemeral nature of all things. What can we really possess, after all? Our realization that there is actually nothing that can be held on to can become a powerful factor in cultivating our inner wealth of generosity, which is a wealth that can never be depleted, a gift that can forever be given, a seamless circle that feeds itself. As the Buddha tells us, "The greatest gift is the act of giving itself."

The Buddha taught "kingly or queenly giving," which means giving the best of what we have, instinctively and graciously, even if none remains for ourselves. We are only temporary caretakers of all that is provided; essentially, we own nothing. As this understanding takes root in us, there is no getting, possessing, and giving; there is just the spaciousness that allows all things to remain in the natural flow of life.

Someone once asked Gandhi, "Why do you give so much? Why do you serve all these people?" Surprisingly, Gandhi answered, "I don't give to anyone. I do it all for myself." The aim—and the fruit—of our dana practice is twofold: we give to help and free others, and we give to help and free ourselves.

Here are some questions we can ask ourselves to help determine if we are giving and receiving with mindfulness:

- What is happening in my body when I give?

- What is happening in my mind?

- Is there a sense of ease, openness, and unsentimental lovingkindness and compassion in my heart, body, and mind?

- Is there a feeling of depletion, weakness, fear, anger, or confusion—a contraction of my heart, body, and mind?

- Can I go beneath my stories, ideals, and beliefs about how I want the exchange to be or not to be, or how I believe it is supposed to be or not supposed to be?

- Can I mindfully recognize when I am caught in stories, beliefs, or wishful or aversive thoughts in relation to generosity?

Mindful attention can also help us to know more clearly how much to give in particular situations—and whether or not it's appropriate to give at all. Here are some questions to consider:

- Am I giving beyond what is appropriate or giving beyond what may be healthy for me emotionally and/or physically?

- Are my heart, body, and mind relaxed, open, and joyful when I feel I've given just enough, or do I experience anguish and contraction of the heart, body, and mind in giving too much?

- Am I aware of when the most generous act might be to step back and simply let people take care of themselves, to let go and allow a particular situation to "just be" and work itself out?

Using these questions as guidelines, we can begin to understand the "middle way" of the Buddha's teaching of dana. Mindfulness is what allows insight to arise in a perfectly natural way and what allows us, in turn, to let go—to recognize ourselves as aspects of the natural flow of life and, in this recognition, to give and receive effortlessly in healthy and wise ways.

Excerpted from "The Gift That Cannot Be Given," Vol. XII, No. 4, Summer 2003

GIVING UP GOSSIP

*Why we gossip and how
practice can help us stop*

by Bhikshuni Thubten Chodron

Gossip has many allures; otherwise we wouldn't enjoy doing it. It has entertainment value, and anyone can participate. But what exactly is it that makes us tingle with excitement when using wrong speech? Do we think we'll shine brighter by exposing another's faults? Or that we'll bond with others through maligning a common outsider? Or will we be empowered, especially if we feel oppressed by someone in authority? These so-called advantages of unskillful speech need to be investigated further.

Gossip can mean many things, from benignly shared information about someone not present to false rumors insidiously spread, to idle chitchat about someone's personal life. The question to ask is, *What is our motivation when we talk about others?* From a Buddhist perspective, the value of our speech depends principally upon the motivation behind it.

When talking about others is motivated by thoughts of ill will, jealousy, or attachment, conversations turn into gossip. These thoughts may seem to be subconscious, but if we pay close attention to our minds, we'll be able to catch them in the act. Many of these are thoughts that we don't want to acknowledge to ourselves, let alone to others, but my experience is that when I become courageous enough to notice and admit them, I'm on my way to letting them go. Also, there's a certain humor to the illogical way that these negative thoughts purport to bring us happiness. Learning to laugh at our wrong ways of thinking can be therapeutic.

How do we begin to notice our motivations? This is where daily meditation practice is essential. Some quiet time alone each day to review our thoughts, feelings, words, and deeds is essential for a healthy lifestyle. For example, when we wake up, we generate our motivation for the day. *Today, as much as possible, I won't harm anyone verbally or physically or even with my thoughts. As much as possible, I will help others in whatever big or small way presents itself. And I'll keep the long-term motivation of becoming enlightened for the benefit of all beings in my heart.* Starting the day with a conscious intention like this transforms all our interactions during the day. In the evening, we again sit quietly and evaluate our day. *How did living according to my motivation go?* When we see shortcomings, we apply one of the Buddha's teachings to transform our motivations and actions. We rejoice at the thoughts, words, and deeds that kept true to our morning motivation. When we're really serious about avoiding gossip, we try to prevent the circumstances for gossip by choosing our companions carefully and being heedful of the topics we discuss with them.

I've found that the best antidote to gossip is deliberately and consistently meditating on the kindness of others and cultivating lovingkindness toward them. Sit down sometime and reflect on everything others have done for you since you were born. Start with your parents or another kind adult who fed you as an infant. Think about all the people who contributed to your education, all those who encouraged you to exercise your talents, and all those who supported you through ups and downs. It's truly amazing how much others have done for us. When our minds become convinced that we've been the recipients of a tremendous amount of kindness in our lives, the wish to speak ill of others vanishes. Instead, we become happy to talk about others' good qualities, virtuous activities, accomplishments, and good fortune. Then not only is our own mind happy but everyone who speaks with us becomes happy as well. The goodness in our hearts overcomes any wish to gossip.

SEVEN TIPS FOR GIVING UP GOSSIP

1. Recognize that gossip doesn't undo the situation you're talking about. It only puts in motion another situation based on negative feelings.

2. Know that comparing yourself to others is useless. Everyone has his or her own talents. In this way, give up jealousy and the wish to put others down.

3. Be aware of and transform your own thoughts, words, and deeds rather than commenting on those of others.

4. Train your mind to see others' positive qualities and discuss them. This will make you much happier than gossiping ever could.

5. Forgive, knowing that people do harmful things because they are unhappy. If you don't make someone into an enemy, you won't want to gossip about him.

6. Have a sense of humor about what you think, say, and do, and be able to laugh at all of the silly things we sentient beings carry out in our attempt to be happy. If you see the humor in our human predicament, you'll be more patient.

7. Practice saying something kind to someone every day. Do this especially with people you don't like. It gets easier with practice and bears surprisingly good results.

Excerpted from "The Truth About Gossip," Vol. XV, No. 4, Summer 2006

CHALLENGES
AT WORK

How to handle conflict skillfully using a
traditional Tibetan Buddhist method

by Michael Carroll

The workplace presents us with some tough challenges that require both professional skill and spriritual wisdom. Giving difficult feedback to a colleague, confronting an offensive boss, motivating a disillusioned coworker, losing a job, exposing a fraud or a petty office theft—such challenges are real and unavoidable aspects of our jobs. Managing such difficulties can make us feel anxious or disillusioned and, at times, even arrogant, inadequate, or fearful.

But navigating such workplace difficulties need not be distressing. In fact, managing conflicts skillfully can be a powerful opportunity for personal and professional growth. What I've found particularly useful is a traditional Buddhist way of working with conflict: the Mahakala method.

Carrying a weapon in each of his four arms, the Tibetan deity Mahakala strikes a threatening pose. But

Mahakala is actually a protector deity, and meditators have long relied on his powers to help them through difficulties of all kinds in their daily lives. He represents our natural ability to promote what is sane and decent and to eliminate what is unreasonable and harmful. His weapons—a medicine-filled skull cup, a hooked knife, a sword, and a trident—represent four inner resources, traditionally called the "four actions," for skillfully working with conflict by pacifying, enriching, magnetizing, and destroying.

Being impulsive or arrogant about what is right and wrong, especially during a conflict, can be disastrous. We may think we're doing what is best for everyone, but often we are only demonstrating our own inflexibility and aggression. Mahakala's fierce pose reminds us to be alert and mindful—to manage conflicts precisely and to act with sanity and decency. Here are the four principles that underlie the Mahakala method.

PACIFYING

Pacifying, represented by the skull cup filled with a calming medicine with magical properties, is our ability to work with conflict peacefully. Often we view business conflicts as confrontations. We tense up, wanting to prove our point or possibly show our coworkers how clever or tough we are. Sometimes we may try to escape the discomfort (and avoid blame) by resorting to excuses or white lies.

Mahakala's pacifying weapon is our ability to drop this struggle altogether. Pacifying starts with acknowledging that our defensiveness is an unnecessary psychological weight that is getting in the way of working with the problem. Rather than focus on winning or losing, we can permit our defensive energy to transform into curiosity about the conflict itself. What is actually at stake here? What does the other person really want to say, to see happen? Why is the other person so upset, and what would eliminate this distress? Listening, asking questions, appreciating the other's point of view, expressing gratitude, and seeking clarification are all pacifying activities.

ENRICHING

Enriching, represented by Mahakala's hooked knife, which transforms raw material into nourishment, is our ability to support and encourage others—even our adversaries. Typically, we protect our own territory in a confrontation, preserving our resources, voicing our opinions, achieving our objectives. When we enrich a conflict, we recognize that we need not limit ourselves to such a narrow view. Providing perspective, seeking options, promoting win/win solutions, offering assistance, revealing commonalities, making concessions, telling stories that clarify a point, building alliances—all these are enriching activities. Once we've employed the first action of pacifying conflict with gentle curiosity, we can promote a sane resolution by inspiring others to feel empowered and supported.

MAGNETIZING

Magnetizing, represented by Mahakala's sword, which focuses attention, is our ability to attract resources during conflicts. Since we are willing to relinquish some of our territory when we enrich the situation, we can now invite others to make concessions, seek alternatives, or trade resources. By its very nature, conflict resolution requires compromise. By modeling our own resourcefulness first, we can then invite others to offer suggestions and share responsibility.

Magnetizing need not be just corporate strategy. The supervisor who inspires employees to work late, offering an extra day off; the police officer who convinces kids to say no to drug dealers, letting them play late-night basketball; even leaving the extra penny at the cashier counter in order to borrow one later—these are all examples of magnetizing.

DESTROYING

The fourth action of Mahakala is destroying, represented by the trident, whose three prongs destroy the three poisons of anger, greed, and delusion with one stroke. Because we have the patience and wisdom first to pacify, enrich, and magnetize, we establish the foundation for being firm and forceful, when and if necessary. Destroying is our ability to say no skillfully and precisely: to walk away from a bad business deal, openly disagree with another's opinion, terminate a floundering project, confront a fraud, or close a struggling company. Destroying is our ability to take a stand—firmly and directly.

When we feel defensive or mistreated during a conflict, we tend to misuse our ability to destroy. Angry words, dismissive attitudes, abrupt and harsh decisions all arise out of a desire to overcome the conflict rather than work with it mindfully. The Mahakala method suggests that we listen first, support others, and seek compromise before we say no—before we say "You're fired" or "The contract is canceled."

Being firm and direct when making tough decisions need not be sloppy and degrading. Because we are willing to listen and compromise, because we are willing to consider options and appreciate others, we can confidently turn down a job offer, challenge a colleague's rude remarks, or simply say, "The price is just too high."

The four actions of the Mahakala method teach us that if our state of mind is not threatened by workplace conflicts, we can take a fresh look at confrontations and be generous in spirit and intention. We can afford to drop our defensiveness and listen to our colleagues; we can afford to be imaginative and open. If we slow down and drop our resistance to work's unpleasantness, we discover that we are resourceful enough to be daring, free from fear and arrogance. Such confidence enables us to know instinctively which situations need to be confronted, which should be nourished, and which can be disregarded. Mahakala reminds us to sharpen up during times of conflict, to be mindful and pay attention. With such alertness we can in fact preserve the sanity of our workplace even during extreme discord. We need not fight the energy of conflict. We can practice the four actions of the Mahakala method and embrace our jobs precisely and authentically.

Excerpted from "Mahakala at Work," Vol. XIV, No. 2, Winter 2004

NDING PATIENCE

How to survive a traffic jam—
on the road or in the heart

by Michele McDonald

When I was a child, I was told many times "Be patient" or "Patience is a virtue." I would relate to these words in much the same way I would to the order "Eat your spinach." To me, "Be patient" meant "Grin and bear it" or that I should repress my feelings about the disagreeable aspects of life. This is not what is meant by patience from the Buddhist perspective, however.

Patience, or *khanti,* is the sixth of the Ten Perfections, or *paramis* (the virtues that one has to perfect in order to fully awaken; there are ten paramis in the Theravada tradition, six paramitas in the Mahayana). The clarity of wisdom and the softness of compassion are the companions of each of the perfections. Patience is motivated by our desire for inward and outward peace and by faith in our ability to accept things as they are. In Buddhism patience has three essential aspects: gentle forbearance, calm endurance of hardship, and acceptance of the truth.

GENTLE FORBEARANCE

The first aspect of patience is gentle forbearance. We may be the exhausted parent of a child who is having a fit over some baffling homework; perhaps patience in this case means taking a few deep breaths instead of yelling in frustration. Or we may be on the verge of making a brilliant retort to a coworker, but we hold our tongue rather than say something hurtful. Even though our impatience is triggered, we can tap into the deeper reservoir of our motivation not to do harm. Gentle forbearance may feel difficult—even contrived—because it doesn't constitute true acceptance of how things are. But it is nonetheless a critical aspect of patience because it helps us restrain ourselves long enough to determine the most skillful action for the moment.

Gentle forbearance helps to anchor our attention in the movement of the breath. Can we truly receive just one breath? Can we sustain the attention from the birth of the breath through its life and through its passing away? We notice that in these moments of attention we are temporarily freed from mental torment. There is no need to focus on our expectations or attachment to results. Impatient thoughts come and go by themselves, just as the breath comes and goes by itself.

Any time we want life to be different than it is, we are caught in impatience. We lose our sense of humor; and self-pity, despair, and blame seep into the heart. Gentle forbearance includes the spirit of forgiveness. When we feel conflict with others, understanding their suffering is the first step in being able to communicate, forgive, and begin again. The practice of forgiveness happens when we are able to realize the underlying cause of our anger and impatience, and this allows us to distinguish between someone's unskillful behavior and essential goodness. Serenity and calm develop as we learn to accept imperfection in others and ourselves.

ENDURANCE OF HARDSHIP

The second aspect of patience is the calm endurance of hardship. The Buddha said that the world rests on suffering. But endurance of suffering doesn't mean doing nothing to alleviate it. Patience isn't passive; it's motivated by an acceptance of and compassion for suffering rather a desire to eradicate it. When we feel impatient with our relationships, our work, or our spiritual practice, we need to realize that we are resisting how things are. A sense of humor and curiosity about our lives can also help us confront impatience.

My five-year-old niece complained to me recently, "I hate school." I replied, "Oh, that's too bad. Why?" "Because it's so boring," she said. She loves the movie *Finding Nemo,* so I reminded her how Dory and Nemo's father, Marlin, endured the obstacles on their long journey to liberate Nemo. I asked, "What did Dory say to Marlin when they were lost and ready to give up?" She remembered, "When life gets you down, just keep swimming." She laughed, and she became interested in exploring why she gets bored in school. I challenged her to tell me one interesting thing that is happening every time she thinks she's bored. Through investigating boredom instead of concluding that we are wasting our time and disconnecting from what is, we can pause, explore, and begin again.

In a frustrating situation, it helps to ask ourselves the question, *What would being patient mean right now?* We can explore what happens to our relationship to our experience when we find ourselves rushing around, always anticipating the next moment, the next event. The more we practice patience, the more time we find we have. Perhaps we've become accustomed to eating so fast we don't even taste our food. Asking ourselves this question slows us down enough to appreciate receiving our food—receiving our life. Gratitude and contentment arise. Many of us try to do so many things at once that there is no space for serenity. We wonder why we are unhappy, why we feel alienated. We just need to remember to practice relaxing into our life, in all its joys and sorrows, and to relinquish the need to know what's going to happen next.

ACCEPTANCE OF THE TRUTH

The third aspect of patience, acceptance of the truth, means that we accept our experience as it is—with all its suffering—rather than how we want it to be. We recognize that because our experience is continually changing, we don't need it to be different than it is. This acceptance of "things as they are" requires profound wisdom and compassion, which take a long time to evolve; we must therefore develop a long-enduring mind that will enable us to understand time from a radically new perspective. As we come to this understanding, we gain the strength to be present for the long haul, and we are less likely to get caught in being overly insistent, frustrated, and demanding.

There is great power in patience because it cuts through arrogance and ingratitude. It is the path that lets us move from resistance to acceptance and spontaneous presence. Holding on to our judgments about others and ourselves is a major cause of impatience. Repeating softly to ourselves "May I be happy just as I am" and "May I be peaceful with whatever is happening" helps us accept our vulnerabilities, imperfections, and losses: everything from chronic physical and emotional pain to the death of loved ones, the end of a job or relationship—even nightmare traffic jams.

By accepting the agreeable and disagreeable aspects of life, we are no longer limited by our longing for life to be different than it is. We have all the time in the world, in the spaciousness of every moment.

"Finding Patience," Vol. XIII, No. 4, Summer 2004

Just Say No

Mindfulness as a means to avoid overeating

by Sandra Weinberg

The Buddha gave many teachings on what to do about distracting thoughts. Certain practices can be adapted to help us when food cravings arise. What is important to remember is that in any moment, we have options; the practice is to find the skillful means for each situation.

Intention is the key; everything else rests on this. We all have different triggers for overeating; know yours. Also keep in mind what your goals are—not to eat, not to go off your diet—and which foods are important for you to avoid. Consider which emotions make you feel the most vulnerable, and when you feel that way, turn to meditation, affirmation, or visualization for support. Then, set and hold the intention not to pick up a trigger food.

Substitute the thought of food with the thought of something more important. For example, visualize the face of someone you love, or feel gratitude for all the gifts you have in your life. Imagine yourself engaged in some pleasurable activity; for example, see yourself on that vacation you're looking forward to. The Buddha taught, "As we think, so we become."

Mentally follow the entire process of giving in to the desire to eat. See the whole cycle from beginning to end. If you take the first bite, where will that lead? What has happened in the past? How will you feel the next day? If, instead, you refrain from eating, how might you feel? Ask yourself, *What do I really want right now? What is the feeling behind the urge for food?*

Stop whatever you are doing at the moment you feel the urge to eat, and do something entirely different: stretch, yawn, get up and walk, make a phone call. Even a simple action can break the trance.

Cultivate willingness to ask for support. In Buddhist practice, we take refuge in the Sangha to support us in our practice. For support in avoiding destructive eating, we can phone a friend who understands our intention, for example, or join a support group for overeaters. On an everyday level, "support" might simply mean asking the waiter to remove the basket of rolls from the table.

Maintain nonjudgment. If you overindulge, don't punish yourself. You will only make your suffering worse. Instead, observe your behavior with a compassionate heart. Then remember the instruction that is the foundation of meditation practice: begin again, with wise intention.

Meditate to reduce craving. Start by taking a few deep breaths. With a half smile on your face, imagine that you are inhaling a sense of calm and exhaling any tension, any thoughts about food. Allow the breath to return to normal. Bring your attention to your belly and the inner sensation of the breath rising and falling in that area. When thoughts of eating or of a specific food come to mind, note, *thought arising.* Become aware of the pleasant or unpleasant feelings that accompany the thought, then shift your attention back to the body, experiencing whatever physical sensations arise. Cultivate moment-to-moment awareness. Not resisting, not forcing. Just this, just this.

Thoughts come and go. Feelings come and go. Allow yourself to experience the transient nature of thoughts and feelings, welcoming everything that arises as just this, not me, not mine.

Adapted from "How to Say No" and "Meditation to Work with Craving," Vol. XII, No. 4, Summer 2003

A Breath of
Fresh Air

*Seven meditations for
connecting with nature*

by Mark Coleman

Since I began leading meditation retreats in nature, I've observed again and again what a profound sense of peace people feel when they spend some meditative time outside in the forest or in open meadows. The power of the natural world encourages us to let go of our habitual mode of being, which is usually self-centered, acquisitive, and endlessly seeking something outside of ourselves. The everyday thinking mind, with its restless concerns and perennial planning, begins to calm down. The body feels more at ease, and the heart slowly opens and resonates with the peace of the natural world. On wilderness meditation retreats, people taste the depth of intimacy it is possible to experience with nature, themselves, and their community.

Nature teaches us simplicity and contentment, because in its presence we realize we need very little to be happy. Since we are part of the animal kingdom, our senses are naturally more alive in the outdoors. The rustle of leaves or the rapid flight of birds could indicate the presence of a mountain lion or bear. Hiking in places where we are not the only predator helps us understand that all of life is intimately interwoven and that we are a part of that web. Meditation training, on the other hand, provides the tools to steady the mind so we can be open to receive the jewels of nature. Through meditation we learn how to work skillfully with thoughts and emotional patterns that interfere with simply being able to rest wherever we are, with full presence.

The following are some exercises to help you connect with the natural world in a meditative way.

BEGINNER'S MIND

Take a walk and let yourself be called to a particular tree. Stay with the tree awhile to study, look, feel, smell, and sense it. Listen to it as wind rustles its branches. Bask in its shade in the midday sun. Get to know it at different times of the day and in different seasons. How is it connected with life around it? How do you get to know it, and which senses do you use?

Feel the difference between your idea of the tree and the rich textural experience of it. Notice the impulse to move on because of impatience, resistance, or boredom. When you feel you know the tree, what does that do to the sense of curiosity and mystery? Can you maintain interest even when you think you have reached the end of your exploration? Is it possible to fully know what a tree really is? Start to bring this curious attention to all that you meet.

SILENCE

Spend a period of time in a quiet place in nature to experience silence. Can you connect with the silence that is there even when there are sounds? What interrupts the experience of silence? Does being in silence create any sense of discomfort? Do you want to distract yourself from it? Does the silence allow your mind and body to rest more in stillness and quiet?

WORKING WITH THOUGHTS

Take some time to sit or walk in nature. Simply be as present as you can. Notice when your attention is lost in thought and how thinking makes you less present to your environment. For a period of time, practice letting go of your thoughts as soon as they arise and returning your attention to what is happening in the physical environment. How does that affect your experience?

LETTING GO OF OUR STORIES

When you are lost or caught up in an emotional storm or contracted in self-centeredness or plagued by obsessive thoughts, notice what happens when you step outside or go for a walk and pay attention to the sky, the air, the light, the movement of wind, the feel of grass under your feet. Be aware of how the spaciousness that can arise allows a natural disidentification with inner turmoil and a regaining of perspective.

KNOWING YOUR BACKYARD

Take some time to investigate the source of your water, food, lumber, firewood. Where do your waste products go? Is the food that you eat grown locally? What are the indigenous animals, birds, plants, and trees in your local area? What are their habitats, where do they nest, eat? What species, what land is currently under threat in your region? Since you are part of this chain of interrelated life, what are you doing that supports or threatens the health of that which may be in danger?

LOVE

Take time to be with something you love in nature that brings out your natural curiosity and delight. It may be a wild iris, the shimmering luminescence of water in a stream, the patterns and colors of a butterfly's wing. Let yourself be drawn to it. Engage your senses. Are you touched by the sense of wonder? Practice daily or weekly, spending time in nature with what most allows your heart to open. How does such love feel in the mind, body, and heart? What effect does it have on your sense of connection with the web of life?

A DAY IN NATURE

Take a day to be alone in nature. Select a location where you are not likely to be interrupted by many people. You can divide the time between periods of contemplative sitting and gentle walks. In sitting meditation, cultivate an open attentiveness toward the present moment. You can focus on the inner experience of breathing and the sensations of the body. Or you can pay attention to the experience that arises from sitting outside—the touch of the breeze on your skin, the physical connection with the earth, the sounds of birds, animals, and the wind, and the fragrances in the air. Try meditating with the eyes open, allowing the eyes to be soft and receptive with a wide field of vision while maintaining awareness of the other senses, especially hearing.

While walking, let go of any goal-orientation. Simply let yourself walk slowly, carefully, with full awareness of the space you are walking in. Let go of any intention to get anywhere. Listen to whatever draws you in the landscape—a particular tree, rock, stream, or a vast open vista. Or perhaps a lizard or beetle draws you into a conversation. Let your senses be wide open and receptive. Give little attention to your thoughts and instead keep turning to your inner and outer environment. If you begin to feel spacey or unfocused, resume sitting meditation, centering attention upon the breath. The less you do outwardly, the more will open to you.

Excerpted from "A Breath of Fresh Air," Vol. XIV, No. 4, Summer 2005

THE WISE
INVESTIGATOR

*Cultivating wisdom by taking an
interest in everyday life just as it is*

An interview with Sayadaw U Tejaniya

TRICYCLE: *You seem to emphasize practicing mindfulness in everyday life as opposed to sitting meditation. Can you say something about that?*

Sayadaw U Tejaniya: This is basically what the Buddha wanted, for people to practice all the time. I'm just advertising the Buddha's words. Sitting meditation can still be part of the practice. I emphasize mindfulness in daily life because people neglect that so much, and it's a very helpful, valid practice—especially when there's not that much time to sit.

What role, then, does sitting meditation play?

I often say that it's not the posture that's meditating; it's the mind. That's how I understand meditation.

How do you define meditation?

It's cultivating good qualities in the mind. It's making conditions right so good qualities can arise. If, while sitting, you're dreaming up things the mind can feel greedy about, I don't call that meditation. That's why I say that the mind working to do the meditation is more important than the posture. But people associate the word "meditation" with "sitting." The two words have become synonymous, but this is a mistake. There are two kinds of meditation. In *samatha* (calm abiding), you need to sit and be still. My emphasis is Vipassana (insight meditation). For Vipassana practice, sitting is not necessary. The purpose of practicing Vipassana is to cultivate wisdom. We cultivate wisdom to understand, to see clearly, to know. You don't remove the defilements; wisdom does.

You've spoken often of the depression you experienced as a layperson and how you got through it. Can you say something about that?

I began practicing at age 14, so long before I experienced depression I'd already developed the ability to regard anything that came up in my mind and deal with it objectively, without getting involved or taking it personally when ugly stuff came up. When I became depressed I could apply all these skills. I've been depressed three times. The first time I made a strong effort, just snapped myself out of it. And the second time, too. But each time the depression came back, and each time it came back stronger. The first two times I overcame depression, my recovery didn't last long. I know now that the first two times I'd used effort but no wisdom, no understanding. During the last depression, I had no energy left in me to make the effort. Depression followed me everywhere.

What did you do?

The key for me in dealing with my depression was right attitude. I realized I'd have to use my wisdom to learn about it, understand it.

How did you do that?

By just recognizing the depression and being present with it. I would just recognize that this was nature, that this was just a quality of mind; it was not personal. I watched it continually to learn about it. *Does it go away? Increase? What is the mind thinking? How do the thoughts affect feelings?* I became interested. I saw that when I'd do the work with interest, my investigation would bring some relief. Before that I'd been at the depression's mercy, but I learned I could actually do something. I was choosing to be proactive, to find out about depression, and then it lightened.

Was it acceptance that changed it?

That was the main thing, complete acceptance. I saw I was helpless to do anything, so I just let it be there. But I could examine it, do something with myself. I couldn't do anything to it, but I could investigate it and come to know it.

Why do you think "interest" was successful while "effort" ultimately failed?

With interest and investigation there's wisdom. Effort alone, without wisdom—the way people generally understand it—is associated with strained activity because it is usually motivated by greed, aversion, and delusion. Effort with wisdom is a healthy desire to know and understand whatever arises, without any preference for the outcome.

Are you using "interest" for right effort?

Right effort is effort with wisdom. Because where there is wisdom, there is interest. The desire to know something is wisdom at work. Being mindful is not difficult. But it's difficult to be continuously aware. For that you need right effort. But it does not require a great deal of energy. It's relaxed perseverance in reminding yourself to be aware. When you are aware, wisdom unfolds naturally, and there is still more interest.

You say that we can cultivate awareness in all our activities. Yet the challenge is great. Can you give a practice that is particularly suited to lay life, one you found useful as a businessman?

For laypeople, speech is a great opportunity to practice. The four precepts of right speech (the precepts cautioning against false speech, malicious speech, harsh speech, and useless speech) gave a real boost to my awareness as a layperson and businessman. Since awareness and wisdom had to come into the picture whenever I spoke, I had to apply them all day.

Saying things you shouldn't say or speaking much more than is necessary brings a lot of agitation to the mind. The other extreme, complete silence, or not speaking up when it is useful or necessary, is also problematic. Applying right speech is difficult in the beginning; it takes practice. But if you practice every time you talk to someone, the mind will learn how to be aware, to understand what it should or should not say, and to know when it is necessary to talk. Of course you will make many mistakes. Every mistake is a learning opportunity that will teach you how to do better next time.

Excerpted from "The Wise Investigator," an interview by James Shaheen, Vol. XVII, No. 2, Winter 2007

PRACTICING
WITH LOSS

Our sorrows provide us with the lessons we most need to learn

by Lama Surya Das

Loss is a fact of life. Impermanence is everywhere we look. We lose loved ones. We lose our health. We lose our glasses. We lose our memories. We lose our money. We lose our keys. We lose our socks. We lose life itself. We have to come to terms with this reality. Sooner or later, all is lost; we just don't always know when it will happen.

We are all going to suffer losses. How we deal with them is what makes all the difference. For it is not what happens to us that determines our character, our experience, our karma, and our destiny, but how we relate to what happens.

Realistically, since we will all suffer many losses, we need better, more evolved and astute ways of approaching sorrow and emotional pain. We need to be more conscious about the ways our losses can help us become wiser and more spiritually evolved; we also need to be more sensitive to and aware of other people's pain and suffering.

With every breath, the old moment is lost, a new moment arrives. This is something Buddhist meditators know. We breathe in and we breathe out. In so doing, we abide in the ever-changing moment. We learn to welcome and accept this entire process. We exhale, and we let go of the old moment. It is lost to us. In so doing, we let go of the person we used to be. We inhale, and we breathe in the moment that is becoming. We repeat the process. This is meditation. This is renewal. It is also life.

MEDITATION ON IMPERMANENCE

Sit someplace where you can be quiet and alone. Try to find a place that brings you closer in touch with a sense of the natural ebb and flow of all life. In Tibet, this kind of meditation is often done outdoors in a charnel ground (boneyard, or burial ground) or beneath clouds moving across the sky, but these particular forms aren't absolutely necessary. You can watch the waves move in and out on a beach; you can sit near a waterfall or in a park. In autumn you can watch leaves flutter to the ground. Other places sometimes suggested to increase awareness of impermanence are the city dump, car junkyard, and hospital entrance.

Wherever you are, get comfortable. Release the muscular tension throughout your body. Breathe in through your nostrils; breathe out through your nostrils. Do this several times until you are feeling relaxed and settled.

Rest in the moment. Stay with this awareness of breathing. Be aware, attentive, and mindful. Let your breath come and go, rise and fall. Simply be with what you are presently experiencing, beyond judgment and beyond interference or alteration. Don't suppress what you feel or what you think, but also don't allow your mind to get carried away into trains of discursive thinking. For the moment, don't try to work or figure anything out. Let it all settle, dissolve, return to where it all arose.

EXERCISE FOR PROCESSING LOSS

Start by listing your greatest losses. Just jot down whatever comes to mind. This is not a test; nothing has to be alphabetized. Skim the surface at first and just see what comes up. Don't worry about whether or not you are writing exquisite prose. In some ways, writing in this way corresponds with the Tantric principle of getting it all out until you are exhausted and then seeing who you are at the bedrock level. Some people are working through a current loss; others are enmeshed and caught up in the past. Start from wherever you are.

After you have skimmed the surface, you might want to consolidate your loss list or break it down into categories, such as "material loss," "relationship loss," "lost opportunities," or "lost dreams," to name just a few possibilities. Which areas stand out for you? With each of your losses, reflect on what happened. Reflect on your deepest feelings and get into the details. When you start writing, you might be surprised at the losses that take priority.

You've learned a meditation technique or two, developed a regular practice, and mastered some methods for carrying mindfulness into daily life. So it's all smooth sailing from here, right?

Not always. You do yourself a disservice if you assume that every time you meditate, you'll achieve perfect harmony and bliss. As Pema Chödrön explains in her Foreword, even the most experienced meditators often encounter physical discomfort and mental distractions when they sit.

Classical Buddhist teachings mention five hindrances, or obstacles, to meditation—five mental states that interfere with concentration and insight: desire; anger or ill will; sleepiness; restlessness or worry; doubt. When these states of mind arise while you're meditating, you have a perfect opportunity to work with them on the spot.

The articles in this section offer practical advice on how to deal with common impediments to practice. In "When in Doubt, Keep Meditating," Sharon Salzberg discusses reinvigorating your faith in meditation. In "Like a Dragon in Water," Roshi Pat Enkyo O'Hara writes about developing steadfastness when distractions pull you off the cushion. For a reader encountering a dry spell in meditation, when it seems as if nothing's happening, Douglas Phillips discusses motivation and what progress in meditation really means ("Going Nowhere?").

With the breath such an important factor in meditation, questions about it often arise. Christina Feldman addresses common concerns in "Receiving the Breath."

Of all the disturbing emotions we experience both on and off the meditation cushion, desire is one of the most prevalent. In "Working with Desire," Matthieu Ricard outlines three different methods, drawn from Tibetan Buddhism, for freeing ourselves from the clutches of desire that's tinged with craving or grasping.

Fear is another major issue for practitioners. When fear arises during meditation, it's a "seminal moment," says Lama Tsony, who offers an antidote in "Facing Fear." In "Inviting Fear," Ajahn Amaro Bhikkhu goes even farther, laying out a technique for deliberately bringing fear into your meditation in order to work it through.

Physical pain is one of the most prevalent distractions for meditators. In "The Wisdom of Discomfort," Sylvia Boorstein provides insight into how modest discomfort can actually deepen practice. For people with back pain who have difficulty finding a comfortable sitting position, Karen Ready offers various suggestions ("Pull Up a Chair"). Certain meditation techniques can even be used to relieve chronic pain, as Jon Kabat-Zinn explains in "Liberating Ourselves from the Prison of Pain."

What if you've hit a wall, and you're thinking of giving up meditating? Read Michael Dairyu Wenger's "Practicing the Five Perfections." He explains why "the perfect time to practice is now" and "the perfect student is you."

WHEN IN DOUBT, KEEP MEDITATING

Q&A with Sharon Salzberg

Question: I make it a point to keep sitting every day, but lately I've been asking myself what good it's doing me, apart from the value of sticking to my commitment and the supposed benefits of spending time in silence and alone. How can I reinvigorate my faith in the practice?

Doubt and faith in our meditation practice often arise and pass away depending on what we are using as criteria for success. The first step is to try to move away from incessantly evaluating what's going on in our practice. We need to be willing to go through ups and downs without getting disheartened. When doubt arises, try to recognize it as doubt and realize that it is a constantly changing state.

If that doesn't help, you might need to seek clarification about the meditation method you're using and perhaps make a change in your practice. You shouldn't hesitate to ask a teacher or fellow practitioner about that. But in most cases, the doubt is simply a reflexive sign of our impatience.

This example is sometimes used to describe practice: It's as though you're hitting a piece of wood with an ax to split it. You hit it 99 times, yet nothing happens. Then you hit it the hundredth time, and it breaks open. But when we're hitting the wood for the thirty-sixth time, it doesn't exactly feel glorious.

It's not just the mechanical act of hitting the wood and weakening its fiber that makes for that magical hundredth moment, just like it's not the physical act of sitting on the cushion that leads to realization—though both are certainly necessary. It's also our openness to possibility, our patience, our effort, our humor, our self-knowledge. These are what we are actually practicing, no matter what happens or doesn't happen to our problems, our moods, our sense of "being in the moment."

Excerpted from "Doubt: Q&A with Sharon Salzberg," Vol. XIII, No. 3, Spring 2004

LIKE A DRAGON
IN WATER

*What to do when distractions
pull us off the cushion*

by Roshi Pat Enkyo O'Hara

Thinking about steadiness in practice reminds me of when I was a little girl and would swim in the great breaking waves of the Pacific coast of Baja California. The surf was ragged and sometimes treacherous, but for those who were accustomed to its rhythms, it was possible to swim through and around the currents, to bob up from under the fiercest waves. I think a key to this ability was sensing that one was part of the ocean and that to play in it was to let go into the wave, sometimes swimming under, sometimes alongside it. There were days when the ocean was utterly calm and days of wild intensity, and for a child, no matter what, there was that fish-like ease and joy of play.

Perhaps most of us enter meditation practice with the hope of finding that kind of natural joy in our lives, in the hopes of experiencing each moment fully, with the freshness of moment-to-moment awareness. And in the initial stages of our practice, many of us manage to find the quiet space that opens us to our spaciousness and spontaneous nature. Buoyed by this experience, our practice gratifies us and propels us along for a while.

And then the inevitable distraction or doubt or difficulty arises. Whether it is a subtle change in our schedule or a disturbing loss of faith, we lose our footing, drop our practice, and often completely forget for weeks at a time that we even had a meditation practice! And it is so difficult to come back, to actually stop and sit down and practice again.

We know that we should "just do it," but our ever-subtle and tricky "monkey minds" make that "should" and that "just" infinitely difficult, even interesting, and distracting. Instead of sitting down on our cushion or going to our meditation center, we think and talk and distract ourselves with all the reasons why not to do it. Or we simply "forget" to practice.

Now if the practice is so good for us, why is it so difficult to maintain a steady practice? It may be that the notion that practice is "good for us" is the very impediment—we all know how we can resist what is good for us at the table, at the gym, and on the Internet. This mechanical notion of practice—*if I practice, then I will be (fill in the blank)*—leads to discouragement because it is not true that practice inevitably leads to happiness or anything that we can imagine. Our lives, like the ocean, constantly change, and we will naturally face great storms and dreary lulls.

How, then, do we put our minds in a space where practice is always there, whether tumultuous or in the doldrums? It requires a completely radical view of practice: practice is not something we do; it is something we are. We are not separate from our practice, and so no matter what, our practice is present. An ocean swimmer is loose and flows with the current and moves through the tide. When tossed upside down in the surf, unable to discern which way is up and which is down, the natural swimmer just lets go, breathing out, and follows the bubbles to the surface.

And so it can be with our practice. Seeing our practice as our life, we just let go and do it. We just practice a steadiness in our daily meditation. Without expectations of any kind, we just practice, day in and day out, through the high points and the low. *I really doubt this practice is helping me. Okay, still, it is time to sit, right through this doubt.* Or, *Oh, I didn't sit all week! Okay, right now I'll sit for 20 minutes.* And each time we come back to our practice, we experience it as more inherent to our lives. Maezumi Roshi, based in Los Angeles, would often use the Spanish expression for "little by little" to indicate this patient quality of practice: "Being one with the practice: you are transformed *poco a poco.*"

This understanding of our practice is expressed by the great 13th-century Japanese Zen teacher Dogen, when he says that our meditation practice "is not step-by-step meditation; it is simply the dharma gate of peace and joy. It is the practice-enlightenment of the Ultimate Way. . . . When you grasp this, you are like a dragon in water or a tiger in the mountains."

"Like a Dragon in Water," Vol. XI, No. 4, Summer 2002

GOING NOWHERE?

Q&A with Douglas Phillips

Question: I'm sitting every day and I feel like I'm not getting anywhere. What should I do?

What motivates you to practice, and is your practice really designed to get you where you want to go? Does this question of getting somewhere arise only in regard to sitting or in other aspects of your life as well? Does it arise from an intelligence that points to something that needs to be changed, or is it indicative of a more chronic tendency toward doubt and self-judgment?

We are often attracted to the dharma because we want something—to be less angry, more relaxed, less fearful, more loving. We want to suffer less and live more expansively, with greater freedom and less constriction. In other words, we quite naturally come to contemplative practice with expectations. It is important to know the difference between the desire/aspiration that gets us to practice and the desire/craving that creates suffering, that unquenchable longing for life to be other than it is. The relationship between *dukkha* (suffering/unsatisfactoriness) and *tanha* (craving/aversion) can be understood as the difference between how my life in this moment actually is and how I want it to be. The greater this difference, the greater the suffering. One may also see that an attachment to expectations arising from these wishes is directly correlated to suffering. Great expectations often lead to great suffering. So what does "progress" on the Great Way look like? How do I generate energy for this practice without creating desire, aversion, or confusion? What should be happening when I sit day after day?

Imbedded in this question of getting somewhere is the assumption that something should be happening other than what is actually happening. Maybe I feel there should be more calmness, less back pain, or certain mystical experiences. I may wish that the image I have of myself as patient, nonreactive, and loving would be how I act when my teenager yells at me or my boss is demeaning or threatening. After all, if I'm sitting like a Buddha, shouldn't I behave like one?

Our practice is to meet life exactly as it is and to notice whatever fear, anger, or doubt gets in the way of direct intimate contact with this moment, bringing attention to that as well. Rather than changing something or seeking to get somewhere we imagine we should be, practice is about seeing clearly exactly how things really are and how we relate to them. Practice thus becomes an increasing intimacy with life just as it is, and there is nothing— including the idea that we should be getting something or somewhere—that is unworthy of the clear, nonjudgmental attention we call mindfulness.

When we have developed a degree of concentration, our work is to then be fully attentive to exactly what is presenting itself in the awareness. This doesn't require profoundly deep concentration states but rather a genuine interest in what is happening right at this moment.

There is no place to get to, no one to become, and nothing to do but bring full attention to the breathing, the tightness in the back, the nervousness in the stomach, the aversion, or whatever else arises. We often imagine that we have to solve or change what is there in our life, when the solution is found in the full attention to just what is here at this moment. The practice of moment-to-moment allowing—bringing full attention to when we are clinging and when we are not—is the practice of liberation. It is this full attention that heals the fragmentation of our lives. Can we begin to notice what happens in moments of clear awareness when we are not so obsessed with changing something or making it go away? What happens when attention and "what is" meet? Can we begin to learn about ourselves by seeing ourselves precisely as we are, not only on the cushion but throughout the day as well?

Full attention is both an activity of learning and the actualization of unconditional love. It is this selfless, choiceless love that heals the illusion of separateness, brokenness, and alienation, yielding a gratification, faith, and confidence not dependent on external or internal conditions beyond our control. Practice-Life is the dynamic activity of bringing full attention to what is presenting itself most clearly in the awareness for as long as it is there, and with deepening simplicity and joy, knowing Just This Much!

Excerpted from "On the Cushion: Q&A with Douglas Phillips," Vol. XII, No. 3, Spring 2003

Receiving
the Breath

Q&A with Christina Feldman

Question: When I try to bring awareness to my breath, I feel instead like I'm interfering with its natural flow. What should I do?

This is not an unusual experience. Throughout our lives, we breathe without effort; then the moment we try to breathe consciously, our breathing suddenly feels blocked, shortened, or constricted. Our bodies know how to breathe without instruction, yet it can feel as if we are having to learn how to breathe all over again.

One reason for this is that you have suddenly become the breather. Your mindfulness of breathing has taken on something extra, a layer of self-consciousness, which brings with it tension and uncertainty. You may be trying too hard. Self-consciousness disguised as mindfulness often manifests as an effort to control the breath. Observe this. There is insight to be gained in seeing how we transfer life patterns of control, anxiety, or self-consciousness into our meditation practice. Learning to undo some of these patterns within our practice is a meaningful step in learning how to release their grip on the rest of our lives.

It is important to remember that there is no "right" breath. If you carry with you the idea that your breath should be deep and full when in reality it is shallow, you immediately get into trouble. At times the breath is deep, at times shallow, at times freely flowing, and at other times it can feel blocked. Your practice is to be with your breath as it is, learning to let go of how you think things should be. Mindfulness of breathing is a practice of learning to harmonize your attention with what is, in this moment. Short, long, deep, shallow are all fine breaths. Trust your body; it knows what is needed.

Some people come into meditation with a history of breathing difficulties such as asthma. The moment they consciously bring their attention to their breath, the emotional history associated with breathing comes to the forefront of their consciousness. They find themselves struggling with the breath in meditation practice just as they have in life. The fear of not having enough breath to sustain life serves to make each breath an increasingly arduous process. Your meditation should be founded in ease and relaxation. If you have historical associations with the breath that hinder its free flowing, it may be helpful to adopt for a time another object of attention, such as listening. Bear in mind that it is the development of attention that is of primary significance; the object of attention is secondary.

As we begin to practice mindfulness of breathing, we often see ourselves initially as the breather, apart and separate from the breath itself. The direction and development of the practice is eventually to bridge this separation until our attention is absorbed fully into the breath. The breath breathes itself, and we experience a place of deep calmness, concentration, and ease. When we breathe, we just breathe. As our practice develops, we learn to let go of much of the emotional and psychological baggage that surrounds so much of what we do in life. Essentially, we learn to let go of the "doer." It is important to be patient with this process. Mindfulness of breathing is a practice of patient intimacy, learning to come closer to the simple process of just breathing.

Without becoming overly strategic or feeling that this is a problem you are required to fix, there are a couple of ways to experiment with letting go of the tension that surrounds your breath. You might experiment with simply focusing your attention in the area of your upper lip and nostrils. Just notice the sensation of your breath entering and leaving your body. Let go of any expectation that your breath should be deeper than it is. Be aware just of the coolness of your incoming breath and the warmth of your outgoing breath. If you notice that there is still tension within your breathing, take your attention just to listening for a few moments. Again, don't look for sounds; just be receptive to the sounds near and far that come to you. Then return your attention to your breathing once more. See if that same quality of receptivity that you brought to listening can be brought into your awareness of breathing. Sense if it is possible just to receive your breath. Your body is breathing; trust it, let it be just as it is.

"On the Cushion: Receiving the Breath," Vol XII, No. 4, Summer 2003

WORKING WITH DESIRE

Three ways of dealing with craving and grasping, drawn from Tibetan Buddhism

by Matthieu Ricard

Buddhism does not advocate the suppression of all desires but rather it offers the means to gain freedom from afflictive emotions. The desire for food when we are hungry, the aspiration for peace in the world, the thirst for knowledge, the wish to share our life with dear ones, or the yearning for freedom from suffering—all of these can contribute to lasting happiness as long as they are not tainted by craving and grasping. Like the other emotions, desire can be experienced either in a constructive or in an afflictive way. It can be the catalyst for a meaningful life—or the maelstrom that wrecks it.

Usually, when a desire arises, we either satisfy or repress it. In the first case, we surrender our self-control; in the second case, a painful conflict builds up. The problem with merely satisfying a desire is that we set into motion a self-perpetuating mechanism: the more salty water we drink, the thirstier we feel. This is how we become addicted to the causes of suffering. But once we know how to have a dialogue with our emotions, the intensity and frequency of the mental images that trigger desire will diminish, and we will become less influenced by desire, without having to repress it in any way. The few images that still arise will be like fleeting sparks in the vast expanse of the mind.

If we lack inner freedom, any intense sensory experience can generate strong attachments that entangle us. On the other hand, if we know how to perfectly maintain our inner freedom, we can experience all sensations within the pristine simplicity of the present moment, in a state of well-being that is free from grasping and expectation.

When desire is particularly intense and is experienced as an affliction, we begin by using antidotes. Two diametrically opposed mental states cannot arise at the same time toward the same object. For example, we cannot wish to harm and benefit another person at the same exact instant, just as we cannot shake someone's hand and give him a punch in the same gesture. The more we generate inner freedom from attachment, the less "room" there will be for craving in our mental landscape. If we use the antidote of nonattachment each time a craving arises, not only will it be effectively counteracted but also the very tendency to crave will gradually erode until it eventually disappears.

The crucial point is to maintain constant vigilance over and awareness of our mental state so that, at the moment that afflictive emotions rise up, they will not trigger a chain of deluded thoughts. Thus, we neither let desire overwhelm our minds, nor do we repress it while leaving it intact in a hidden corner of the mind. We simply become free from its alienating power.

In the second method, instead of trying to counteract every afflictive emotion with a particular antidote, we act on a more fundamental level and use a single antidote to deal with all afflictions. If we examine our emotions and trains of thought without suppressing their natural activity, we find that they are nothing but dynamic streams devoid of intrinsic existence. So, instead of trying to block desire, we can simply examine its true nature. In such a practice, we focus our attention on desire itself, rather than on its object. Does desire have any shape or color? Where does it come from? Where does it dwell? Where does it go when it vanishes from the mind? Is it burning us like a fire or pulling us like a rope? All we can say is that desire arises in the mind, stays in it for a while, and dissolves in it. The more we try to find any intrinsic characteristics in desire, the more it melts away under our gaze, as frost under the morning sun.

In Buddhism this is called liberating desire by recognizing its empty nature. By doing so, we deactivate its power to cause suffering. Once we have gained some degree of experience, this liberation will happen spontaneously and effortlessly, like the dissolution of a drawing made with the finger on the surface of water. In this way, thoughts will no longer perpetuate in an obsessive stream. Rather, they will cross the mind like birds passing through space, without leaving any trace.

The third method is the most subtle and difficult. If we carefully examine our emotions, we discover that, like musical notes, they have various harmonics. Just as anger has an aspect of clarity, desire has a component of bliss that is distinct from craving. If we know how to distinguish these aspects, it becomes possible to experience a blissful state of mind without being affected by the deluded aspect of grasping. We become aware that emotions are not intrinsically afflictive but only become so when we identify with them and grasp onto them.

Such a practice, however, requires great skill in the language of emotions and is not free from dangers: To let powerful emotions express themselves without falling prey to them is like playing with fire. If one succeeds, one will greatly progress in understanding the nature of mind; if one fails, one is enslaved by the ordinary ways of experiencing desire.

The different methods to get free from destructive emotions are like keys: it does not matter whether a key is made of iron, silver, or gold, as long as it opens the door to freedom. The question is not which approach is superior to the others but which one fulfills for us the essential goal of the path of inner transformation. When we suffer from a particular ailment, the best medicine is not the most expensive one but the one that works best.

"Working with Desire," Vol. XIII, No. 4, Summer 2004

FACING FEAR

Q&A with Lama Tsony

Question: Lately I've been dealing with a lot of fear during my meditation practice. It seems to come from nowhere, and it either focuses on a specific attachment or manifests as a more existential, nameless sort of thing. How can I deal with this?

Fear is what happens when reality collides with our personal fiction. Our practice is based on expectations—expectations about who we are, why we are practicing, and what our practice should be. As our hope disintegrates, it may be replaced by fear. Our characteristics, personality, all of our beautiful plans and ideas are like snowflakes about to fall on the hot stone of our meditation practice.

Maybe you've poked through boredom and have had a first taste of spaciousness. Until your experience has become stable, the fear remains that your dreams, your life, and your base could fall apart. The more you contemplate space, the more you are aware of the dissolution of everything you have assumed to be real, lasting, and reliable—including your motivation and your practice. Now it all feels transitory and unreliable. This crisis, rooted in dissolution, translates as fear.

This is a seminal moment in our practice. Each time it manifests, each time we are aware of fear, we have a choice: we can acknowledge our problem and work with it, or we can run away from it and seek refuge elsewhere—distractions, pharmaceuticals, weekend feel-good-about-yourself workshops, whatever. We are free to refuse the disappointment and the dissolution. We don't have to put ourselves back into the situation where the foundation of our being is shaken by the experience of impermanence and emptiness.

But if we decide to continue, if we're convinced of the sanity of the Four Noble Truths and decide to take refuge in the dharma that the Buddha taught, we need to be courageous. We can choose to take refuge in the brilliant sanity of enlightenment, the Buddha; trust the process of the path, the Dharma; and rely on the experience of those who guide us along the path, the Sangha. We can choose to explore our mind, learn about its problem areas and hidden treasures, but it won't be comfortable. The guidance of a spiritual friend or teacher is crucial at this stage of our practice.

At the same time, we can be nice to ourselves, accept ourselves as we are, and let go of what we are pretending to be. Our crisis is a normal phase. We all enter the spiritual path as ego-based beings, and as such we have ego-based hopes and fears. Practice is virtually never what we expect. We feel like we've got it all wrong, thinking, *The more I meditate, the worse I become.* My teacher, Gendun Rinpoche, always responded to this by saying, "When you see your own shortcomings, it's the dawn of qualities. If you only see your qualities, there's a problem."

It's true that if we continue to try to create our personal nirvana through our practice, we're going to suffer even more. If we use the practice tools that develop intelligence and clarity with a confused, selfish motivation, reality is bound to collide with our fiction. This is where practice is *supposed* to bring us. This is the proof that the dharma works. It's the end of our confused, fictive world—and the dawning of truth.

When fear arises within our meditation, we apply an antidote. Recognizing what is happening at each instant as mind, we remain in the present. It is important to remember that patterns don't have to repeat themselves. Through remaining in the present, we can let go of the past and the future—the headquarters of our fears. We recognize and then we let go, whether coming back to the focal point of our meditation—posture, breath, visualization—or nonconceptual space. Through motivation, honesty, and confidence, we can practice with our fears and go beyond them in a way we never thought possible.

"Facing Fear," Vol. XVI, No. 1, Fall 2006

INVITING FEAR

A meditation for taming
fear with attention

by Ajahn Amaro Bhikkhu

There are many ways to meditate on fear. One is to wait until it appears adventitiously. Another is to invite it in—when we send out invitations we can be a little better prepared for who shows up at the party.

Perhaps for both methods of approach the first thing to bear in mind is that fear is not the enemy, it is nature's protector; it only becomes troublesome when it over-steps its bounds. In order to deal with fear we must take a fundamentally noncontentious attitude toward it so that it's not held as "My big fear problem" but rather as "Here is fear that has come to visit." Once we take this attitude, we can begin to work with fear.

Begin by sitting quietly and focusing the attention as clearly as possible on the present moment, using a simple tranquil object to establish equilibrium. The nat-ural rhythm of the breath, moving in the empty space of the heart, is, for most people, good for this purpose.

Once such centeredness has been established, delib-erately bring to mind something that will arouse a fear reaction. For example: anthrax in the mail, nuclear war, suicide bombers. Or any other memory, imagined possibility, or image that triggers the compulsive effect.

Once the seed crystal has been dropped into the mental pool and the consequent flow of thoughts and images has begun, make a definite and concerted effort to withdraw the attention from the stories the thoughts are telling. Bring it instead into the sensations of the physical body:

- Where do I feel the fear?
- What is its texture?
- Is it hot or cold?
- Is it painful? Rigid? Elastic?

We are not necessarily looking for verbal answers to all these questions, rather we are just trying to find the feeling, accept it completely and not add anything to it. Just noting, *fear feels like this.*

Many find that fear locates itself primarily in the solar plexus, sitting like a tightened knot in the belly. Just feel it, know it, open the heart to it as much as possible. We're not trying to pretend or force ourselves to like it, but it is here—right now it's the way things are.

Let this process run for at least 10 minutes, then consciously let it wind down—not suppressing it but, as when it's time for guests to leave, making hints and letting the event wind down naturally. It might take a while, but that's fine; just let it run out at its own pace. During this time, reestablish the breath as a focal point and use the exhalation to support the fading of the fear-wave.

Once it has come to an end, focus the attention on the feeling of the breath, moving as before in the empty space of the heart. Let the heart be clearly conscious that the fear cycle has come to cessation: it arose out of emptiness, returned to emptiness. It was florid and impactful in its appearance, but the overarching quality, now having been seen directly, is its transiency.

The effect of this practice is to train the heart, so that when the next wave of fear arises, from whatever quarter, something in us knows. The intuitive wisdom faculty is awakened and recognizes, *I know this scenario— don't panic—it looks impressive but it's just the fear reaction.* It becomes vastly easier to avoid being sucked into the vortex of anxiety. The feeling is not pleasant, but the heart knows, with absolute certainty, *it's only a feeling.* And if action needs to be taken, then that action will be motivated by wisdom, kindness, and sensitivity to time and place rather than by neurotic reactivity and habit.

Excerpted from "Inviting Fear," Vol. XI, No. 3, Spring 2002

THE WISDOM
OF DISCOMFORT

Q&A with Sylvia Boorstein

*Question: What should I do if I experience considerable
physical pain in my knees and my back when I practice
sitting meditation?*

One way to address concern about pain is to ask
three basic questions: How does sitting in a particular
way increase the ability of the mind to see more clearly?
How does seeing more clearly develop wisdom? And
how does wisdom lead to compassion? (It is, after all,
wisdom and compassion, not stalwart sitting, that are
the point of practice.)

So, how does sitting still, upright, and resisting the
temptation to move, focus and clear the mind? First,
holding a styled position requires attention—attention
brought to bear on the present situation—so random
thoughts are less likely to distract the mind. Second,
the decisiveness in the mind that intends to be awake
and present—"I'm doing this now"—also guards against
distraction. And third, the mind itself, in a context of
simplicity, has the natural tendency to return to ease.
(I often think about the snow globes with lovely scenes

at their center, scenes hidden from view as long as the "snow" is shaken up. Once the globe is left alone on a steady surface, the snow settles, and what is meant to be seen is revealed.)

What we most frequently see when the mind is focused and clear are the habits of mind that create unnecessary suffering, habits fueled by greed and hatred and delusion. Over and over we struggle with our lives, resenting our experiences, blaming ourselves for not being other than who we are. We are unable to see past the immediate, overwhelming drama of our personal story to find relief—indeed, liberation—in the consoling realization of an astonishingly lawful cosmos. Paying attention to current experience stops the stories that create and recreate suffering.

The practice of seeing clearly is what finally moves us toward kindness. Seeing, again and again, the infinite variety of traps we create for seducing the mind into struggle, seeing the endless rounds of meaningless suffering over lusts and aversions (which, although seemingly urgent, are essentially empty), we feel compassion for ourselves. And then, quite naturally, we feel compassion for everyone else. We know as we have never known before that we are stuck, all of us, with bodies and minds and instincts and impulses, all in a tug-of-war with our basic heart nature that yearns to relax into love. Then we surrender. We love. We laugh. We appreciate.

So much for philosophy. Here is some additional, practical advice. Do try to find a position in which you can sit still. Then, even if modest discomfort arises in the body, sitting through it allows for the discovery that the mind can relax and manage discomfort. Sitting with modest discomfort teaches the mind to be less frightened. Experiencing the disappearance of discomfort soothes the mind, makes it confident, and allows for the insight of impermanence: everything passes. Even the most comfortable positions—like the most comfortable lives—become uncomfortable after a while. That's a lesson, too.

Here is a final, important, technical instruction: when the discomfort you feel is significant, move. Adjust your posture. You want your mind to be focused and alert, but not hysterical. When the level of discomfort is past the level at which the mind can maintain its balance, it is no longer useful. Rather than a cause for the arising of insight, the discomfort becomes the cause of dismay and doubt and disappointment. Much better to stretch your body, relax, and start again.

Excerpted from "The Wisdom of Discomfort: Q&A with Sylvia Boorstein," Vol. XI, No. 4, Summer 2002

LIBERATING
OURSELVES FROM
THE PRISON OF PAIN

*$\mathscr{H}$ow meditation can help
us cope with chronic pain*

An interview with Jon Kabat-Zinn

Tricycle: What is pain and how can meditation help us deal with it?

Jon Kabat-Zinn: Physical pain is the response of the body and the nervous system to a huge range of stimuli that are perceived as noxious, damaging, or dangerous. There are really three dimensions to pain: the physical, or sensory component; the emotional, or affective component—how we feel about the sensation; and the cognitive component—the meaning we attribute to our pain.

Let's say you've got a pain in your back. You can't lift your children; getting in and out of the car is difficult; you can't sit in meditation. Maybe you can't even work. That's the physical component. But you're having to give up a lot, and you're going to have feelings about that—anger, probably—and you're susceptible to depression. That's the emotional response. And then you have thoughts about the pain—questions about what caused it, negative stories about what's going to happen. Those expectations, projections, and fears compound the stress of the pain, eroding the quality of your life.

There is a way to work with all this, based on Buddhist meditative practices, that can liberate you, to a very large extent, from the experience of pain. Whether or not you can reduce the level of sensory pain, the affective and cognitive contributions to the pain—which make it much worse—usually can be lessened. And then, very often, the sensory component of the pain changes as well.

You mean that once you've changed your relationship to the pain, the physical discomfort may decrease?

That's the key point: you change your relationship to the pain by opening up to it and paying attention to it. You "put out the welcome mat." Not because you're masochistic but because the pain is there. So you need to understand the nature of the experience and the possibilities for, as the doctors might put it, "learning to live with it," or, as the Buddhists might put it, "liberation from the suffering." If you distinguish between pain and suffering, change is possible. As the saying goes, "Pain is inevitable; suffering is optional."

There have been studies looking at how the mind processes acute pain at the sensory level. Subjects are randomized between two groups, then given the cold pressor test, where a tourniquet is placed around your biceps, then you stick your arm into ice water. There's no more blood flow, so your arm gets very painful very fast. They measure how long you can keep your arm in the water as a function of whether you are given an attentional strategy, such as paying attention to the sensations and really moving into them and being with them as nonjudgmentally as you can—a mindfulness strategy, in other words—or a distraction strategy, where you just try to think about other things and tune out the pain. What they found was that in the early minutes of having your arm in the ice water, distraction works better than mindfulness: you're less aware of the discomfort because you're telling yourself a story, or remembering something, or having a fantasy.

But after the arm is in the cold water for a while, mindfulness becomes much more powerful than distraction for tolerating the pain. With distraction alone, once it breaks down and doesn't work, you've got nothing.

The eight-week Mindfulness-Based Stress Reduction program you designed uses the body scan as well as sitting meditation to manage pain. Would you explain how the body scan works?

The body scan is a variation on a traditional Burmese practice called sweeping, from the school of U Ba Khin. S. N. Goenka teaches it in his 10-day Vipassana retreats. The traditional method involves tuning in to sensation in a narrow horizontal band that is slowly brought down through the entire body, as if you were giving yourself a CAT scan. This is analogous to the way certain metals, such as zinc, are purified in a circular zone furnace. I thought it would be hard for people in chronic pain to sit for 45 minutes, so I modified the practice. It is done lying down, starting at the toes and moving up through different regions of the body.

This practice is a way of getting out of the head and developing intimacy with the body. The challenge is, can you feel the toes of your left foot without wiggling them? You tune in to the toes, then gradually move your attention to the bottom of the foot and the heel, and feel the contact with the floor. Then you move to the ankle and slowly up the leg to the pelvis. Then you go to the toes of the right foot and move up the right leg. Very slowly you move up the torso, through the lower back and abdomen, then the upper back and chest, and the shoulders. Then you go to the fingers on both hands and move up the arms to the shoulders. Then you move through the neck and throat, the face and the back of the head, and then right on up through the top of the head.

And all the while, you're in contact with the breath. I tend to have people feel the breath moving in and out of the body region they're attending to, so that there's a sort of dual awareness. As you move up the body, you're learning how to focus on a particular region, then let go of it and move on. It's like cultivating concentration and mindfulness simultaneously, because there is a continual flow. You're not staying with one object of attention.

What if your pain is so bad that it's hard for you to concentrate on anything else?

You have a number of choices. Let's say you have lower back pain. You can say, "I'm going to try to focus on my toes, even in the presence of back pain. The back's always there; I'll get to it sooner or later. Why don't I see if I can really learn to focus my attention where it's being asked to focus?" Often, when you do that, the felt sense of the pain in the back lessens.

But if the pain is too great, you can go to the region where the pain is and let the breath merge with it. Breathe in and feel the breath, or in your mind's eye see the breath moving down into the lower back. Then on the out-breath, as the breath lets go, see if you can allow the mind to let go. You're not trying to shut off the sensations from the lower back—just to experience the fullness of whatever happens as you let go.

Then in the next moment, the sensations and the feelings and the thoughts might all come flooding back, and you've got the next in-breath to work with. So it's a practice.

You develop an observer's attitude toward the pain?

Basically, you're intentionally bearing witness to the pain rather than distancing yourself from it; we're not teaching mindfulness as a dualistic practice. Nevertheless, there's a sense that there's the pain, and there's the observing of the pain. It's important to understand that as an intermediate step toward ultimate liberation. It means that I can rest in awareness, and then ask myself, *is the awareness in pain in this moment?* And the answer invariably is, *as I look at it right now, the awareness of the pain is not in pain.* When you realize you can rest in this awareness, the pain may be just as intense, but you're now cultivating equanimity and clear comprehension. You're seeing the pain as it is, as sensation. There is a knowing that it is not pleasant. But the interpretation that the pain is killing me, or ruining my life, and all the emotions and stories that go with that, are seen for what they are. In that seeing, they often go into abeyance.

What do you tell people who say, "My practice isn't working; I'm still in pain"?

When you think that your practice should be working, then you've already fallen out of your practice and into expectations that the practice is going to achieve some kind of prefigured, desirable result. This need *to get rid of* is its own form of ignorance, and we need to look at our "I" statements. Worthy objects of attention and inquiry are: *Who is suffering? Who is in pain?* We can ask that, but rather than coming up with an answer *qua* thought, we can drop into *not-knowing* and experience simply being aware.

Not that "simply being aware" is easy. When pain arises, the same challenge occurs as when the breath arises. That's one reason to practice when we're not in a lot of pain—to cultivate strong practice so we can rely on it when it becomes extremely difficult to practice.

You seem to be saying that pain is just like the rest of life, only more so.

If you pay attention to the little episodes of pain in your life, you can learn how to work with the bigger episodes because you learn about *anicca,* impermanence; *anatta,* non-self; and *dukkha,* suffering. The meditation orientation is not about fixing pain or making it better. It's about looking deeply into the nature of pain— making use of it in certain ways that might allow us to grow. In that growing, things will change, and we have the potential to make choices that will move us toward greater wisdom and compassion, including self-compassion, and thus toward freedom from suffering.

Excerpted from "At Home in Our Bodies," an interview by Joan Duncan Oliver, Vol. XII, No. 2, Winter 2002

PULL UP A CHAIR

*Practical advice for meditators
with chronic back pain*

by Karen Ready

*Question: I have chronic back trouble and haven't yet
found a position for meditation that I can bear for
more than 10 minutes. I've tried just about everything,
from a* seiza *[meditation bench]* to *zafus, zabutons,
and* gomdens *[types of meditation cushions], in various shapes and degrees of firmness—nothing seems to
work for me. I know some teachers write that pain is
part of the process, but I just can't seem to get past the
physical agony.*

It's true that the priority of cushion sitting is apparent
almost wherever you look. The Buddha himself spoke of
"the case where a monk, having gone to the wilderness,
to the shade of a tree, or to an empty building, sits down
folding his legs crosswise, holding his body erect, and
setting mindfulness to the fore" (*Anapanasati Sutta, Majj-
hima Nikaya* 118). The 13th-century master Eihei Dogen,
in his *Rules for Zazen*, notes, "There are examples from

the past of sitting on a diamond seat and sitting on a flat stone covered with a thick layer of grass," but he goes on to instruct, "When sitting zazen, wear the *kashaya* [ritual robe] and use a round cushion."

All honor to Dogen, and all respect as well to those teachers who tell us that pain is a normal stage in learning to sit or a valuable challenge to meet. Meditation teacher Bodhipaksa instructs, "As you use the breath to soften resistance to the pain or discomfort, you may notice how the experience of pain is in fact a constantly changing mass of different sensations. Experience how it comes into being and passes away moment by moment."

Yet those who have long-term or chronic back pain may need more in the way of material support to really get started or to escape an off-and-on practice with its accompanying feelings of guilt and discouragement. If pain regularly makes you cut meditation short or makes you dread sitting altogether, it's time to try something new. The system offered here uses a chair rather than a cushion:

- Sit on a straight chair, not one where the seat angles back (as many do). If you can, get a couple of wooden blocks, about an inch thick. Place one under each of the back legs of the chair so that you are very slightly angled forward. If you don't have blocks, two small paperback books will do.

- To ensure that you don't lean against the back of the chair, and to support the base of the spine, use something firm but pliable

205

to act as a wedge-support. It can be a small
rolled-up towel, or a small pillow, or even a
hard plastic binder, tucked under the back
of the buttocks at the base of the spine. You
will know that the angle of the body is right
when you are sitting upright and at rest.

Perhaps the most difficult part of this approach
is letting go of your attachment to the idea of sitting
like everyone else, especially during group practice (on
a retreat, for example), where it seems to be assumed
that everyone will bring a cushion and sink onto the
mat at the right moment. We don't like to stick out, and
the self-criticism that can follow is one of the heaviest
impediments there is to attaining any real inner alignment. As a first step, why not try these steps at home
for a week or two to see whether they make a difference
for you as you explore how, with your body just as it is,
you can approach sitting meditation positively and with
increasing confirmation of its profound value.

Adapted from "On the Cushion: Have a Seat," Vol. XVII, No. 2, Winter
2007

Practicing the Five Perfections

*The real work of meditation is practicing
right here, right now, just as you are*

by Michael Dairyu Wenger

Master Dogen, the 13th-century founder of Soto Zen in Japan, was asked by a student, "What should you do if you find yourself in an argument? Should you try to win the argument or should you concede, even though you feel you're right?" Dogen advised neither path. Become disinterested, he told the student, and the argument will lose its energy. The same advice can be applied to feelings of competitiveness in practice: let go of your attachment to appearances of one who wins or has "got it right."

Practice just with what is happening in this moment, with your thoughts and sensations, your discomfort or your wandering mind—in other words, with whoever you are, right here, right now. This is the real work. Are you making your best effort? The practice of the Five Perfections can help us realize this idea.

1. *The perfect time to practice is right now*—not tomorrow or next week or when you're less busy, but right now. Nothing is lacking now: the dharma gate is wide open. All the "if onlys" in the world are just excuses that keep you from meeting this moment.

2. *The perfect place to practice is right where you are*— not in an ashram in India or in a monastery in Japan or in a different meditation center in your town. You can always compare. Instead, practice right here, in earnest!

3. *The perfect teaching is the one before you.* Richard Baker Roshi once told of a dream he had: He was trying to find the answer to a question, and the telephone rang. He ignored the phone and focused instead on the question. On the thirtieth ring he picked up the phone, and the answer came to him through the receiver. What he had labeled a distraction was really the point.

4. *The perfect teacher is whoever is in front of you.* It's a real relationship, not an objective measure of who is the best. You may learn more from a teacher who has faults and who practices with them.

5. *The perfect student is you.* You have within you all the ingredients you need to practice. You are in charge, and once you realize this, you will seek—and find—all the help you need. This is the most important of the Five Perfections.

Sometimes, though, comparing yourself with others can actually be helpful. There comes a point in practice when you have changed the things that are easy to change within yourself, but the more fundamental changes remain. When you feel that you have hit a wall in your practice and don't notice any obvious progress, you can find encouragement in the growth you observe in your fellow practitioners and realize that you, too, may be growing subtly.

Again, *who is it who compares?* The more you can come to see everyone as yourself, the more you will be able to use everything around you to learn about who you are and the more you will be able to transform yourself and be an occasion for everyone else's transformation. We are all sentient beings, and we are all capable of experiencing one another's salvation. If you are only involved in protecting your small self, you are in constant peril!

Excerpted from "On the Cushion: Competing with the Incomparable," Vol. XIV, No. 2, Winter 2004

PART VI

Staying
WITH IT

You're meditating regularly, and you've learned to deal with pain, distraction, and other obstacles to practice that arise. Now what?

Your practice continues. Day by day, week by week, month by month, as you meditate, your practice will deepen and change. Yes, there will be times you avoid your meditation cushion. Maybe it's a cold morning when the alarm goes off early and you don't want to leave the warmth of your bed. Or an evening when you'd rather watch a video or go dancing with friends. Maybe you've got an early appointment or your children's carpool. Staying with your meditation practice doesn't mean giving up your life—far from it: regular meditation takes you deeper into your life, as your motivations become clearer and easier to see. What staying with it requires is a commitment to yourself to find time to meditate, no matter what. If making a long-term commitment seems overwhelming, think of meditation as a commitment you renew each time you sit. And if you skip a day, you don't give up altogether. Just as you do when your mind wanders during meditation, you simply resume practicing. You begin again.

There are many little tricks meditators use to motivate themselves and stick with it. "Meditator's Toolbox" contains 21 of these suggestions, all road-tested by experienced practitioners. They range from being patient with yourself, to experimenting with your breathing and posture, to using a timer or stick of incense to measure your sitting period so you won't keep peeking at the clock.

This is also a good time to consider joining a meditation

group; you'll receive vital support and encouragement from the sangha, or community of practitioners. Working with a teacher is another time-honored, even essential, way to deepen your practice. But staying with your practice isn't just a matter of tricks to keep you seated on the cushion. Above all, there is the power of practice itself to keep you coming back. The Buddha taught meditation as an essential part of the path to liberation, but he didn't save all the pleasures for the end. As Thanissaro Bhikkhu explains ("The Joy of Effort"), "Even though the path requires effort, it's an effort that keeps opening up new possibilities for happiness and well-being in the present moment." And if you stick with it, mastering meditation as you would any other skill, it will lead you all the way to nirvana—to "a happiness totally unconditioned, free from the constraints of space and time."

As Pema Chödrön wrote in the Foreword, "Meditation ultimately helps us say yes to life—and to play like a raven in the wind."

MEDITATOR'S
TOOLBOX

*wenty-one tips to power your practice from
twenty-one experienced meditators*

Bodhidharma tore off his eyelids. Jack Kornfield's teacher told him to meditate at the edge of a well. The Buddhist tradition is full of stories of practitioners who have found unique techniques for stimulating and maintaining their practice. In fact, anyone who has sat on a *zafu* more than once has probably come up with a trick or two for staying there. To tap into this resource, we asked seasoned Buddhist teachers and longtime practitioners to share their favorite meditating tools.

1. JUST GET IN THE POSTURE

Try making a commitment to getting into the meditation posture at least once a day. You don't have to sit for any particular length of time, just get on the cushion. A lot of times, the hardest part is getting there. Once you're sitting down, you think, "I might as well sit for a few minutes," and more often than not, you're getting full sessions in.

— Insight Meditation Society co-founder Joseph Goldstein

2. REFLECT ON THE BIG PICTURE

The breath is not only a useful object of concentration but also a sign of life. A little reflection can bring a sense of gratitude and delight to each breath, which is further enhanced by sensing what the Indian mystic and poet Kabir called "the breath within the breath," the mystery that is riding along on each inhale and exhale.

— Author and meditation teacher Wes Nisker

3. USE A TIMER

When you sit in meditation, use a timer instead of a clock. If you have to keep opening your eyes to check on the time, restlessness can be exacerbated. By using a timer, one frees oneself from the concept of time and discovers a deepening of relaxation and a sense of the timeless.

— Cambridge Insight Meditation teacher Narayan Liebenson Grady

4. GET YOUR PRIORITIES STRAIGHT

If meditation is a priority, then it's helpful to take that word literally and put meditation first. An example would be my rule of not turning on the computer before I've meditated. Simple, but effective. Probably the most trenchant advice I ever heard was in eight words from Suzuki Roshi, "Organize your life so you can sit well."

— Senior Shambhala teacher David Schneider

5. BE PATIENT

When you plant seeds in the garden, you don't dig them up every day to see if they have sprouted yet. You simply water them and clear away the weeds; you know that the seeds will grow in time. Similarly, just do your daily practice and cultivate a kind heart. Abandon impatience and instead be content creating the causes for goodness; the results will come when they're ready.

— Tibetan Buddhist nun and author Bhikshuni Thubten Chodron

6. PLAY WITH POSTURES

Even though we generally refer to meditation as "sitting," when you find that hard to do, you can also "sit" lying down. When I wake up at night with insomnia, I pay attention to the breath or do lovingkindness practice. One year, I could only get myself to "sit" by lying on the ground in the backyard, sensing the layers of the earth, and listening to the sounds of a garden in the city.

— Barbara Gates, co-editor of the journal Inquiring Mind

7. MAKE A VOW

Don't give yourself a choice. Don't ask yourself, *do I want to get up and do this?* You will think of a million other things to do. Just set your alarm and get up and meditate—no questions. It also helps to make a vow. Try promising the Buddhas that you'll meditate every day for a month and see what happens.

— Tibetan Buddhist nun and author Ani Tenzin Palmo

217

8. USE INCENSE

Time a stick of incense. Once you know how long it takes to burn, you can use it to determine the length of your sessions.

— *Tricycle* founder Helen Tworkov

9. WIDEN YOUR PRACTICE FIELD

Don't put arbitrary limits on the field of practice. Trying to live graciously, reading and reflecting wisely, appreciating virtue in others, not making those around you miserable, being a *mensch*—practicing in this way, which is pretty traditional, there is never a lack of opportunity. As for sitting meditation itself—that's something we do for others, so that maybe we can have a more generous spirit and be less of a pain in the neck.

— *Tricycle* editor-at-large Andrew Cooper

10. STILL THE MIND IN UNUSUAL POSITIONS

I like to interpret what the Buddha said when he talked about the four postures suitable for meditation—seated, standing, walking, and lying down—as an invitation to watch the mind in any position, any place, any time. I begin my practice periods with a breathing practice from my teacher Mingyur Rinpoche, then I get into a yoga posture and stay in it for some time. Working in this way, I can watch my mind play around with discomfort, effort, desire, and aversion. Plus, I receive the benefits of the pose by staying in it longer.

— Vajra Yoga founder Jill Satterfield

11. SIT WITH OTHERS

Find others to sit with. Sometimes showing up for others is easier than showing up for yourself.

— *Tricycle* editor and publisher James Shaheen

12. MAKE THE RIGHT DECISION

Every practitioner I know who has been able to continue to practice for years has had to deal with their resistance to sitting. It seems that when we hurl ourselves in a particular direction with vigor and intention, we are also creating a shadow of resistance at the same time. This matter is resolved over time by the decisions we make in the immediate situation: Do we watch TV or sit? Do we schedule a date with a friend during our usual sitting time? Do we skip our sangha night when our parents visit or do we ask them to join us (or excuse us)? Deciding to sit over and over again through every possible seduction establishes the vigor of our intention.

— Russian River Zendo teacher Darlene Cohen

13. EXPERIMENT WITH THE BREATH

My teacher, Than Geoff, has always reminded me that when the mind is fighting the meditation, ask it, "What kind of breath would feel really good right now?" It tricks you into experimenting with the breath, and usually the breath becomes interesting enough and pleasurable enough that concentration can settle in.

— *Tricycle* contributing editor Mary Talbot

14. DRINK COFFEE

Some people say that it was actually Buddhist monks who discovered coffee. The story goes that they were wandering around in the forest somewhere when they came across the beans. They started chewing them and thought, "These are great. We can use this energy for our meditation practice." If you are going to get up in the morning and sit, it doesn't have to be first thing. Get up and have a cup of coffee if it helps. It's when you start taking out the newspaper and doing other stuff that you lose the freshness of mind you have when you first wake up. But if you can have coffee without turning on your cell phone, go for it.

— Downtown Meditation Community teacher Peter Doobinin

15. SIT BECAUSE YOU NEED TO

I'd say to meditators pretty much what Rilke said to poets, "Don't do it unless you have to!" In my little experience, any other motivation than necessity demeans meditation to a conceit, another tool for ego-consolidation of one form or another. Not for nothing is the first point of the Big B[uddha]: There is SUFFERING. That's the one and only actual gate.

— *Tricycle* contributing editor Eliot Fintushel

16. DON'T CHEAT

If you're counting the breaths, for example, don't let it be Enron style. An honest accounting works wonders for the spiritual bottom line.

— *Tricycle* contributing editor Mark Magill

17. TUNE UP BY READING SOMETHING YOU LOVE

I don't mean a text that you're studying—you don't want to encourage the mind to cogitate. Near the place where you like to sit, keep a little selection of readings that inspire happiness or quiet; they can be from any tradition. Recently I've had by my side Thomas Merton's *Thoughts in Solitude,* the *Avadhuta Gita,* and a folder of short poems and quotations from past issues of *Tricycle* and other sources. For a session when the mind is really stirred up, here's a wonderful quote to put it in pause mode, from the mind training teachings in *The Great Path of Awakening:*

> When I am in this kind of mood
> My mat is by far the best place to be.
> This present mental state is fine.
> Moreover, by putting up with this unpleasantness,
> I won't be born in the hell realms. How wonderful!
> I won't be baked or roasted. How wonderful!

— *Tricycle* copyeditor Karen Ready

18. CHECK IN BEFORE YOU START

Once you sit down, in addition to doing a quick scan of your body for tension, take a moment to look at your heart and mind before you "start" officially. Sure, maybe you just rolled out of bed, but what is your mood like—annoyed? Excited (or anxious) at the prospect of a new day? Is your brain still in slo-mo, or was it jolted into a panic by the alarm clock? It can be good to notice where you are before you start counting breaths.

— *Tricycle* contributing editor Andrew Merz

19. HAVE FAITH

Seek the support of a Power Beyond the Self. Dogen says, "Throw body and mind into the house of Buddha, so that all is done by Buddha." If we rely only upon our own resources in trying to develop a meditation practice, we will quickly exhaust ourselves. It is important to know that the Buddha himself supports us in all kinds of ways, some easy to recognize (through the teaching passed down from master to disciple, for instance) and some not. Some of those supports become visible to us only when we believe in the Buddha. Belief in Buddhahood as a Power Beyond the Self can encourage us when nothing else seems to work. That statue on your altar isn't just a decorating idea.

— *Tricycle* contributing editor Clark Strand

20. DON'T PUSH

There's an old Zen saying, "When you sit Buddha, you kill Buddha." Whatever else it might mean about blowing away preconceptions or that kind of thing, it always stuck with me as a very friendly reminder not to try too hard or push too hard; don't try to be a Buddha when you're sitting.

— *Tricycle* webmaster Philip Ryan

21. END CAREFULLY

When you end your meditation, be very careful with how you open your eyes. Try to maintain your center inside rather than letting it flow outside. Then, maintaining your center, get up from the cushion and keep the center inside as long as you can. As my teacher Ajaan Fuang instructed, "When you start out sitting in meditation, it takes a long time for the mind to settle down, but as soon as the session is over you get right up and throw it away. It's like climbing a ladder slowly, step by step, to the second floor, and then jumping out the window."

— Metta Forest Monastery Abbot Thanissaro Bhikkhu

"Meditator's Toolbox," Vol. XVII, No. 1, Fall 2007

THE JOY OF EFFORT

*The Buddha's path doesn't save
all its pleasure for the end—nirvana.
You can enjoy it now.*

by Thanissaro Bhikkhu

When explaining meditation, the Buddha often drew analogies with the skills of artists, carpenters, musicians, archers, and cooks. Finding the right level of effort, he said, is like a musician's tuning of a lute. Reading the mind's needs in the moment—to be gladdened, steadied, or inspired—is like a palace cook's ability to read and please the tastes of a prince.

Collectively, these analogies make an important point: meditation is a skill, and mastering it should be enjoyable in the same way mastering any other rewarding skill can be. The Buddha said as much to his son, Rahula: "When you see that you've acted, spoken, or thought in a skillful way—conducive to happiness while causing no harm to yourself or others—take joy in that fact and keep on training."

Of course, saying that meditation should be enjoyable doesn't mean that it will always be easy or pleasant.

Every meditator knows it requires serious discipline to sit with long, unpleasant stretches and untangle all the mind's difficult issues. But if you can approach difficulties with the enthusiasm that an artist approaches challenges in her work, the discipline becomes enjoyable. Problems are solved through your own ingenuity, and the mind is energized for even greater challenges.

This joyful attitude is a useful antidote to the more pessimistic attitudes that people often bring to meditation, which tend to fall into two extremes. On the one hand, there's the belief that meditation is a series of dull and dreary exercises allowing no room for imagination and inquiry: simply grit your teeth, and at the end of the long haul your mind will be processed into an awakened state. On the other hand, there's the belief that effort is counterproductive to happiness, so meditation should involve no exertion at all: simply accept things as they are—it's foolish to demand that they get any better— and relax into the moment.

While it's true that both repetition and relaxation can bring results in meditation, when either is pursued to the exclusion of the other, it leads to a dead end. If, however, you can integrate them both into the greater skill of learning how to apply whatever level of effort the practice requires at any given moment, they can take you far. This greater skill requires strong powers of mindfulness, concentration, and discernment, and if you stick with it, it can lead you all the way to the Buddha's ultimate aim in teaching meditation: nirvana, a totally unconditioned happiness, free from the constraints of space and time.

That's an inspiring aim, but it requires work. And the key to maintaining your inspiration in the day-to-day work of meditation practice is to approach it as play—a happy opportunity to master practical skills, to raise questions, experiment, and explore. This is precisely how the Buddha himself taught meditation. Instead of formulating a cut-and-dried method, he first trained his students in the personal qualities—such as honesty and patience—needed to make trustworthy observations. Only after this training did he teach meditation techniques, and even then he didn't spell everything out. He raised questions and suggested areas for exploration in the hope that his questions would capture his students' imagination, so they'd develop discernment and gain insights on their own.

We can see this in the way the Buddha taught Rahula how to meditate. He started with the issue of patience. "Meditate," he said, "so that your mind is like the earth. Disgusting things get thrown on the earth, but the earth isn't horrified by them. When you make your mind like the earth, neither agreeable nor disagreeable sensory impressions will take charge of it."

Now, the Buddha wasn't telling Rahula to become a passive clod of dirt. He was teaching Rahula to be grounded, to develop his powers of endurance, so that he'd be able to observe both pleasant and painful events · in his body and mind without becoming engrossed in the pleasure or blown away by the pain. This is what patience does. It helps you sit with things until you understand them well enough to respond to them skillfully.

To develop honesty in meditation, the Buddha taught Rahula a further exercise. "Look at the inconstancy of events in body and mind," he said, "so that you don't develop a sense of 'I am' around them." Here the Buddha was building on a lesson he had taught Rahula when the boy was seven years old. "Learn to look at your actions," he had said, "before you do them, while you're doing them, and after they're done. If you see that you've acted unskillfully and caused harm, resolve not to repeat the mistake. Then talk it over with someone you respect."

In these lessons, the Buddha was training his son to be honest with himself and with others. And the key to this honesty is to treat your actions as experiments. Then, if you see the results aren't good, you're free to change your ways.

This attitude is essential for developing honesty in your meditation as well. If you regard everything—good or bad—that arises in the meditation as a sign of the sort of person you are, it will be hard to observe anything honestly at all. If an unskillful intention arises, you're likely either to come down on yourself as a miserable meditator or to smother the intention under a cloak of denial. If a skillful intention arises, you're likely to become proud and complacent, reading it as a sign of your innate good nature. As a result, you never get to see whether these intentions are actually as skillful as they seemed at first glance.

To avoid these pitfalls, you can learn to see events simply as events and not as signs of your innate Buddha-ness or badness. Then you can observe these events honestly, to see where they come from and where they lead. Honesty, together with patience, puts you in a better position to use the techniques of meditation to explore your own mind.

The primary technique the Buddha taught Rahula was breath meditation. The Buddha recommended 16 steps in dealing with the breath. The first two involve straightforward instructions; the rest raise questions to be explored. In this way, the breath becomes a vehicle for exercising your ingenuity in solving the problems of the mind and exercising your sensitivity in gauging the results.

To begin, simply notice when the breath is long and when it's short. In the remaining steps, though, you train yourself. In other words, you have to figure out for yourself how to do what the Buddha recommends. The first two trainings are to breathe in and out sensitive to the entire body, then to calm the effect that the breath has on the body. How do you do that? You experiment. What rhythm of breathing, what way of conceiving the breath calms its effect on the body? Try thinking of the breath not as the air coming in and out of the lungs but as the energy flow throughout the body that draws the air in and out. Where do you feel that energy flow? Think of it as flowing in and out the back of your neck, in your feet and hands, along the nerves and blood vessels, in your bones. Think of it coming in and out every pore of your skin. Where is it blocked? How do you dissolve the blockages? By breathing through them? Around them? Straight into them? See what works.

As you play around with the breath in this way, you'll make some mistakes—I've sometimes given myself a headache by forcing the breath too much—but with the right attitude the mistakes become a way to learn how the impact of your perceptions shapes the way you breathe. You'll also catch yourself getting impatient or frustrated, but then you'll see that when you breathe through these emotions, they go away. You're beginning to see the impact of the breath on the mind.

The next step is to breathe in and out with a sense of refreshing fullness and a sense of ease. Here, too, you'll need to experiment both with the way you breathe and with the way you conceive of the breath. Notice how these feelings and conceptions have an impact on the mind and how you can calm that impact so the mind feels most at ease.

Then, when the breath is calm and you've been refreshed by feelings of ease and stillness, you're ready to look at the mind itself. You don't leave the breath, though. You adjust your attention slightly so that you're watching the mind as it stays with the breath. Here the Buddha recommends three areas for experimentation: notice how to gladden the mind when it needs gladdening, how to steady it when it needs steadying, and how to release it from its attachments and burdens when it's ready for release.

Sometimes the gladdening and steadying will require bringing in other topics for contemplation. For instance, to gladden the mind you can develop an attitude of infinite goodwill or recollect the times in the past when you've been virtuous or generous. To steady the mind when it's been knocked over by lust or to reestablish your focus when you're drowsy or complacent, you can contemplate death, realizing that death could come at any time and you need to prepare your mind if you're going to face it with any finesse. At other times, you can gladden or steady the mind simply by the way you focus on the breath itself. For instance, breathing down into your hands and feet can really anchor the mind when its concentration has become shaky. When one spot in the body isn't enough to hold your interest, try focusing on the breath in two spots at once.

The important point is that you've now put yourself in a position where you can experiment with the mind and read the results of your experiments with greater and greater accuracy. You can try exploring these skills off the cushion as well: How do you gladden the mind when you're sick? How do you steady the mind when dealing with a difficult person?

As for releasing the mind from its burdens, you prepare for the ultimate freedom of nirvana first by releasing the mind from any awkwardness in its concentration. Once the mind has settled down, check to see if there are any ways you can refine the stillness. For instance, in the beginning stages of concentration you need to keep directing your thoughts to the breath, evaluating and adjusting it to make it more agreeable. But eventually the mind grows so still that evaluating the breath is no longer necessary. So you figure out how to make the mind one with the breath, and in that way you release the mind into a more intense and refreshing state of ease.

As you expand your skills in this way, the intentions that you've been using to shape your experience of body and mind become more and more transparent. At this point the Buddha suggests revisiting the theme of inconstancy, learning to look for it in the effects of every intention. You see that even the best states produced by skillful intentions—the most solid and refined states of concentration—waver and change. Realizing this induces a sense of disenchantment with and dispassion for all intentions. You see that the only way to get beyond this changeability is to allow all intentions to cease. You watch as everything is relinquished, including the path. What's left is unconditioned: the deathless. Your desire to explore the breath has taken you beyond desiring, beyond the breath, all the way to nirvana.

But the path doesn't save all its pleasures for the end. It takes the daunting prospect of reaching full awakening and breaks it down into manageable interim goals—a series of intriguing challenges that, as you meet them, allow you to see progress in your practice. This in and of itself makes the practice interesting and a source of joy.

At the same time, you're not engaged in busywork. You're developing a sensitivity to cause and effect that helps make body and mind transparent. Only when they're fully transparent can you let them go. In experiencing the full body of the breath in meditation, you're sensitizing yourself to the area of your awareness in which the deathless—when you're acute enough to see it—will appear.

So even though the path requires effort, it's an effort that keeps opening up new possibilities for happiness and well-being in the present moment. And even though the steps of breath meditation eventually lead to a sense of disenchantment and dispassion, they don't do so in a joyless way. The Buddha never asks anyone to adopt a world-negating—or world-affirming, for that matter—frame of mind. Instead, he asks for a "world-exploring" attitude, in which you use the inner world of full-body breathing as a laboratory for exploring the harmless and clear-minded pleasures the world as a whole can provide when the mind is steady and clear. You learn skills to calm the body, to develop feelings of refreshment, fullness, and ease. You learn how to calm the mind, to steady it, gladden it, and release it from its burdens.

Only when you run up against the limits of these skills are you ready to drop them, to explore what greater potential for happiness there may be. In this way, disenchantment develops not from a narrow or pessimistic attitude but from an attitude of hope that there must be something better. This is like the disenchantment a child senses when he has mastered a simple game and feels ready for something more challenging. It's the attitude of a person who has matured. And as we all know, you don't mature by shrinking from the world, watching it passively, or demanding that it entertain you. You mature by exploring it, by expanding your range of usable skills through play.

"The Joy of Effort," Vol. XVII, No. 4, Summer 2008

CONTRIBUTORS

Ajahn Amaro Bhikkhu ("Inviting Fear," page 191) is a monk in the lineage of Ajahn Chah and the Thai forest tradition. He is co-abbot of Abhayagiri Monastery in northern California.

James Baraz ("Awakening Joy: A Guided Meditation," page 82) is a founding teacher of Spirit Rock Meditation Center, where he coordinates the Community Dharma Leader program and is teacher-advisor for the Kalyana Mitta network and the Family and Teen Programs. His book *Awakening Joy* will be published in 2009.

Martine Batchelor ("A Refuge into Being," page 72) spent 10 years as a Buddhist nun in Korea. She is a member of the teaching council at Gaia House in England and leads meditation retreats worldwide with her husband, Stephen. Her books include *Women in Korean Zen* and *Let Go: A Buddhist Guide to Breaking Free of Habits.*

Frank Jude Boccio ("Breath and the Body," page 115) has been studying and practicing yoga and Buddhism since 1975, and is the author of *Mindfulness Yoga.* A member of the Tiep Hien Order of Interbeing founded by Vietnamese Zen master Thich Nhat Hanh, he was ordained as a dharma teacher in 2007 by Korean Zen master Samu Sunim. He maintains a private counseling practice in Tucson, Arizona.

Sylvia Boorstein ("Focusing on the Breath," page 66; "The Wisdom of Discomfort," page 194) has been teaching vipassana and *metta* meditation since 1985. A psychotherapist and a founding teacher of Spirit Rock Meditation Center in Woodacre, California, she has a particular interest in daily life as spiritual practice. Her books include *Pay Attention, for Goodness' Sake; Don't Just Do Something, Sit There;* and *Happiness Is an Inside Job: Practicing for a Joyful Life.*

Michael Carroll ("Challenges at Work," page 141) is a teacher in the Kagyu-Nyingma and Shambhala traditions of Tibetan Buddhism, and a consultant with more than 20 years' experience as a human resources executive. Author of *Awake at Work* and *The Mindful Leader,* he lectures widely and conducts seminars on mindfulness in the workplace.

Pema Chödrön (Foreword, page xi) is a leading exponent of meditation teachings applied to daily life. An American-born Tibetan Buddhist nun ordained by the 16th Karmapa, she was a student of Chögyam Trungpa until his death in 1987. Active in establishing Tibetan Buddhist monasticism in the West, she has been abbess of Gampo Abbey in Cape Breton, Nova Scotia, since 1984. Her books include *The Wisdom of No Escape; When Things Fall Apart; The Places That Scare You;* and *Practicing Peace in Times of War.*

Bhikshuni Thubten Chodron ("Giving Up Gossip," page 137) is an American Buddhist nun and student of His Holiness the Dalai Lama. Having been resident teacher at Amitabha Buddhist Centre in Singapore and Dharma

Friendship Foundation in Seattle, Washington, in 2003 she founded Sravasti Abbey, a Buddhist monastic community in eastern Washington. Her books include *Taming the Mind; Working with Anger;* and *Buddhism for Beginners.*

Mark Coleman ("A Breath of Fresh Air," page 154) has practiced Buddhist meditation since 1984. He has been teaching Vipassana retreats since 1997 and also leads wilderness retreats, including backpacking and kayaking throughout the western United States, Alaska, and Baja California. He is the author of *Awake in the Wild.*

Lama Surya Das ("The Heart of Meditation," page 5; "Simply Being," page 11; "Bowing," page 126; "Practicing with Loss," page 164) is a priest and spiritual master in the Nyingmapa School of Tibetan Buddhism, as well as a leading spokesperson for Buddhism in the West. Founder and spiritual director of the Dzogchen Center in Cambridge, Massachusetts, he is also an author, poet, translator, and chantmaster. His books include *Awakening the Buddha Within; The Big Questions;* and *Buddha Is As Buddha Does.*

Peter Doobinin ("Awakening, Step by Step," page 112) is the guiding teacher at the Downtown Meditation Community in New York City. A graduate of the Spirit Rock Community Dharma Leaders program, he is a cofounder of New York Insight Meditation Center.

Christina Feldman ("Receiving the Breath," page 181) is a cofounder of Gaia House in England and a guiding teacher of the Insight Meditation Society in Barre, Massachusetts. Author of several books on meditation, she has been leading insight meditation retreats since 1976.

Gil Fronsdal ("May We All Be Happy," page 75) holds a Ph.D. in Buddhist Studies from Stanford University and has trained in both the Zen and Vipassana traditions. A member of the Teachers Council at Spirit Rock Meditation Center in Woodacre, California, he is founder and primary teacher of the Insight Meditation Center in Redwood City, California.

S. N. Goenka ("Finding Sense in Sensation," page 93) is a lay teacher of vipassana meditation in the tradition of the Venerable Ledi Sayadaw. A former businessman, he was a student of the late Burmese master Sayagi U Ba Khin and in 1974 founded the Vipassana International Academy, Dhamma Giri, near Bombay, India. His popular nonsectarian 10-day meditation course is taught in more than 90 countries, by a network of over 700 teachers he has trained.

Joseph Goldstein ("Cultivating a Daily Meditation Practice," page 16; "Posture, Posture, Posture," page 18; "The Meditation Challenge," page 39) began studying Buddhist meditation in Asia in the late 1960s, and has been teaching Vipassana and *metta* retreats worldwide since 1974. A cofounder and guiding teacher of the Insight Meditation Society and Forest Refuge in Barre, Massachusetts, he helped establish the Barre Center for Buddhist Studies. He is the author of *One Dharma; The Experience of Insight; Insight Meditation;* and *A Heart Full of Peace.*

Narayan Liebenson Grady ("The Refuge of Sitting," page 13) is a guiding teacher at the Cambridge Insight Meditation Center in Cambridge, Massachusetts, and teaches regularly in Barre, Massachusetts, at the Insight

Meditation Society and the Barre Center for Buddhist Studies. She is the author of *When Singing, Just Sing: Life as Meditation.*

Bhante Henepola Gunaratana ("Wisdom Arising," page 64) is a Sri Lankan monk, world-renowned meditation teacher, and founding abbot of the Bhavana Society in West Virginia. He is the author of a classic meditation manual, *Mindfulness in Plain English,* as well as a companion volume, *Eight Mindful Steps to Happiness,* and an autobiography, *Journey to Mindfulness.*

Will Johnson ("Full Body, Empty Mind, page 107) is director of the Institute for Embodiment Training in British Columbia, Canada. His books include *The Posture of Meditation; Aligned, Relaxed, and Resilient;* and *Yoga of the Mahamudra.*

Jon Kabat-Zinn ("Liberating Ourselves from the Prison of Pain," page 197) is professor emeritus at the University of Massachusetts Medical School and founder of its Center for Mindfulness in Medicine, Health Care, and Society and its world-renowned Stress Reduction Clinic. A longtime practitioner of Buddhist meditation and hatha yoga, he has focused on clinical applications of mindfulness throughout his career and is the author of numerous scientific papers. His eight-week Mindfulness-Based Stress Reduction (MSBR) program, described in *Full Catastrophe Living,* is taught in medical facilities worldwide. His other books include *Coming to Our Senses* and *Wherever You Go, There You Are.*

Alexandra Kaloyanides ("The Meditation Challenge," page 39) is *Tricycle's* managing editor.

Cyndi Lee ("Yoga for Meditators," page 22) has practiced hatha yoga and Tibetan Buddhist meditation for over 20 years. Founder and director of OM Yoga in New York City and co-creator of the *OM Yoga in a Box* series, she teaches workshops and retreats worldwide. She is the author of *OM Yoga: A Guide to Daily Practice* and coauthor with her husband, David Nichtern, of *Yoga Body, Buddha Mind.*

Barry Magid, M.D. ("Zen, or Just Sitting" page 69) is a psychiatrist, psychoanalyst, and Zen teacher in New York City. Founder of Ordinary Mind Zendo, he received transmission from Charlotte Joko Beck in 1999. He is the author of *Ordinary Mind* and *Ending the Pursuit of Happiness,* as well as numerous articles on the interface between Buddhism and psychology.

Michele McDonald ("Finding Patience," page 146) has taught insight meditation for 27 years. A guiding teacher of Vipassana Hawaii, she has taught extensively throughout the United States and regularly teaches in Canada, Burma, and elsewhere around the world.

Andrew Merz ("Full Body, Empty Mind," page 107) is a *Tricycle* contributing editor.

Wes Nisker ("Evolution's Body," page 99) is a San Francisco Bay-area journalist, founder and co-editor of the Buddhist journal *Inquiring Mind,* and a meditation teacher associated with Spirit Rock Meditation Center in Woodacre, California. His books include *The Best of Inquiring Mind* (with Barbara Gates); *Crazy Wisdom; Buddha's Nature;* and *The Big Bang, the Buddha, and the Baby Boom.*

Roshi Pat Enkyo O'Hara ("Like a Dragon in Water," page 175) is abbot of Dotoku-ji/Village Zendo in New York City and co-spiritual director of the Zen Peacemaker Order. A priest in the Soto Zen tradition, she studied with John Daido Loori Roshi and the late Taizan Maezumi Roshi. In 1997, she received dharma transmission from Roshi Bernie Glassman.

Douglas Phillips ("Going Nowhere?" page 178) has practiced Zen and Vipassana for more than 30 years. He is the guiding teacher of the Empty Sky Vipassana Sangha in Newton, Massachusetts, and West Cornwall, Connecticut, and a psychologist in private practice.

Reginald Ray ("Earth Breathing," page 96) co-founded, with his wife, Lee, the Dharma Ocean Foundation, a study and retreat center in Crestone, Colorado. A senior teacher in the Shambhala tradition of Chögyam Trungpa, he is a professor of Buddhist studies at Naropa University in Boulder, Colorado, and the author of several books, including *Indestructible Truth* and *Secret of the Vajra World*.

Karen Ready ("Pull Up a Chair," page 204) is *Tricycle*'s copy editor. She served as copy chief on Macmillan's *Encyclopedia of Religion* and has edited scholarly works and spiritual teachings.

Matthieu Ricard ("Working with Desire," page 184) is a Buddhist monk, photographer, author, and translator who holds a doctorate in molecular biology from the Institut Pasteur in Paris and now resides at Shechen Monastery in Nepal. His many books include *Happiness:*

A Guide to Developing Life's Most Important Skill; *The Quantum and the Lotus*, co-authored with Trinh Xuan Thuan; *The Monk and the Philosopher*, co-authored with his father, Jean-François Revel; the photography books *Tibet: An Inner Journey* and *Motionless Journey*; and translations of numerous Buddhist texts.

Marcia Rose ("Cultivating Generosity," page 133) is the founding and guiding teacher of The Mountain Hermitage and founding teacher of Taos Mountain Sangha, both in Taos, New Mexico. She also teaches in Barre, Massachusetts, at the Insight Meditation Society and Forest Refuge.

Sharon Salzberg ("Cultivating a Daily Meditation Practice," page 16; "Posture, Posture, Posture," page 18; "The Meditation Challenge," page 39; "When in Doubt, Keep Meditating," page 173) began studying Buddhist meditation in India in 1971 and has been teaching insight and lovingkindness meditation worldwide since 1974. She is a cofounder of the Insight Meditation Society, Barre Center for Buddhist Studies, and Forest Refuge, all in Barre, Massachusetts. Her books include *Faith; Lovingkindness; A Heart as Wide as the World;* and *The Force of Kindness.*

James Shaheen (Preface, page xv; "The Wise Investigator," page 159) is the editor and publisher of *Tricycle: The Buddhist Review.* He has practiced vipassana meditation since 1996, studying at the Insight Meditation Society and Barre Center for Buddhist Studies in Barre, Massachusetts, and has also practiced with numerous Tibetan and Zen teachers. He is a member of the American Society of Magazine Editors and serves annually as a judge for the National Magazine Awards. A former board member of the Independent Press Association, he has been active in supporting independent media for many years.

Judith Simmer-Brown ("Giving and Taking," page 79) is a prominent Buddhist scholar and author, and a professor of religious studies at Naropa University in Boulder, Colorado. She is a senior dharma teacher in the Shambhala Buddhist tradition founded by Chögyam Trungpa.

Clark Strand ("Worry Beads," page 83) is a *Tricycle* contributing editor and former Zen monk. His books include *Meditation Without Gurus* and *How to Believe in God (Whether You Believe in Religion or Not)*.

Sayadaw U Tejaniya ("The Wise Investigator," page 159) began his Buddhist training as a teenager in Burma, under the late Shwe Oo Min Sayadaw. After a business career and life as a householder, he was ordained as a monk in 1997. He teaches meditation at Shwe Oo Min Dhamma Sukha Tawya in Rangoon.

Thanissaro Bhikkhu (Geoffrey DeGraff) ("The Joy of Effort," page 224) is an American Buddhist of the Thai forest tradition and the abbot of Metta Forest Monastery near San Diego, California. His publications include translations of Ajaan Lee's meditation manuals; *Handful of Leaves,* a multi-volume anthology of sutra translations; *The Wings to Awakening,* an anthology from the Pali canon; and *Buddhist Religions: A Historical Introduction.*

Lama Tsony ("Facing Fear," page 188) was the head of the monastic community at the Dhagpo Kundreul Ling hermitage in Auvergne, France, for 15 years. Now he travels throughout the United States and Europe, teaching Buddhism and leading meditation retreats.

Sandra Weinberg ("Just Say No," page 151) has studied and practiced mindfulness meditation for more than 25 years. She is a cofounder of New York Insight Meditation Center and a graduate of the Spirit Rock Community Dharma Leaders program. A psychotherapist and addictions expert, she leads retreats and workshops on understanding addiction and recovery from a Buddhist perspective.

Michael Dairyu Wenger ("Practicing the Five Perfections," page 207) has practiced at the San Francisco Zen Center since 1972, and helps with dharma group support for groups in the Suzuki Roshi lineage.

ABOUT THE EDITOR

Joan Duncan Oliver is *Tricycle*'s reviews editor and an award-winning journalist whose work has appeared in such publications as *The New York Times, O: the Oprah Magazine, Health, Shambhala Sun,* and *The Best Buddhist Writing 2005.* Her books include *Happiness; Good Karma;* and, most recently, *Coffee with the Buddha.* She has practiced Buddhist meditation for 30 years, studying with teachers in the Zen, Vipassana, and Tibetan Buddhist traditions.

$\mathcal{A}$CKNOWLEDGMENTS

Over the years, *Tricycle*'s editors have talked about publishing an anthology of articles from the magazine, but it took Patricia Gift, our editor at Hay House, to make those vague dreams a reality. A deep bow to Patty, true bodhisattva of the project, and to her assistant Laura Koch and the rest of the Hay House team who brought *Commit to Sit* to fruition.

There would be no *Tricycle* anthology, however, without the vision and dedication of Helen Tworkov, the magazine's founder and for 10 years its editor and guiding force. In launching the first Buddhist publication in the West unaffiliated with any teacher or school, Helen offered leading thinkers of our day an open forum in which to explore Buddhist practice, engage in dharma dialogue, and bring ancient and contemporary teachings to life for an ever-growing audience. A deep bow to Helen—along with our immeasurable gratitude for her commitment to making Buddhism accessible to a wide audience.

Bows also to the 40 contributors represented in *Commit to Sit,* for their inspired and thoughtful writing. Given the hundreds of articles, interviews, dharma talks, and practice pieces *Tricycle* has published since 1991, selecting only a handful was a daunting task. We bow to the dozens of writers whose fine work could not be included here but continues to enliven *Tricycle*'s pages.

Bows to the 21 teachers and practitioners—including several *Tricycle* staff members and contributing editors— who generously shared their secrets for deepening the meditative experience in the chapter titled "Meditator's Toolbox." And to *Tricycle* managing editor Alexandra Kaloyanides, contributing editor Andrew Cooper, and Thanissaro Bhikkhu, bows for helpful input along the way.

And finally, a deep bow to Pema Chodron, who contributed the preface to *Commit to Sit*. A friend and supporter of *Tricycle* from the beginning, she remains a powerful model of how meditation practice can inform, enrich—and indeed, transform—our lives.

Notes

Notes

NOTES

Notes

NOTES

NOTES

Notes

Notes

Notes

Notes

NOTES

HAY HOUSE TITLES OF RELATED INTEREST

YOU CAN HEAL YOUR LIFE, the movie,
starring Louise L. Hay & Friends
(available as a 1-DVD program and an expanded 2-DVD set)
Watch the trailer at: **www.LouiseHayMovie.com**

*ALL YOU EVER WANTED TO KNOW FROM HIS HOLINESS
THE DALAI LAMA ON HAPPINESS, LIFE, LIVING, AND
MUCH MORE.* Conversations with Rajiv Mehrotra.

*FOLLOWING SOUND INTO SILENCE:
Chanting Your Way Beyond Ego into Bliss,*
by Kurt (Kailash) A. Bruder, Ph.D., M.Ed.

*THE GURU OF JOY: Sri Sri Ravi Shankar &
the Art of Living,* by François Gautier

*IN MY OWN WORDS: An Introduction to
My Teachings and Philosophy,*
by His Holiness The Dalai Lama; edited by Rajiv Mehrotra

All of the above are available at your local bookstore,
or may be ordered by contacting Hay House (see last page).

We hope you enjoyed this Hay House book. If you'd like to receive a free catalog featuring additional Hay House books and products, or if you'd like information about the Hay Foundation, please contact:

Hay House, Inc.
P.O. Box 5100
Carlsbad, CA 92018-5100

(760) 431-7695 or **(800) 654-5126**
(760) 431-6948 (fax) or **(800) 650-5115 (fax)**
www.hayhouse.com® • **www.hayfoundation.org**

Published and distributed in Australia by: Hay House Australia Pty. Ltd., 18/36 Ralph St., Alexandria NSW 2015 • *Phone:* 612-9669-4299 *Fax:* 612-9669-4144 • www.hayhouse.com.au

Published and distributed in the United Kingdom by: Hay House UK, Ltd., 292B Kensal Rd., London W10 5BE • *Phone:* 44-20-8962-1230 • *Fax:* 44-20-8962-1239 • www.hayhouse.co.uk

Published and distributed in the Republic of South Africa by: Hay House SA (Pty), Ltd., P.O. Box 990, Witkoppen 2068 • *Phone/Fax:* 27-11-467-8904 • orders@psdprom.co.za • www.hayhouse.co.za

Published in India by: Hay House Publishers India, Muskaan Complex, Plot No. 3, B-2, Vasant Kunj, New Delhi 110 070 • *Phone:* 91-11-4176-1620 • *Fax:* 91-11-4176-1630 • www.hayhouse.co.in

Distributed in Canada by: Raincoast, 9050 Shaughnessy St., Vancouver, B.C. V6P 6E5 •*Phone:* (604) 323-7100 *Fax:* (604) 323-2600 • www.raincoast.com

Tune in to **HayHouseRadio.com®** for the best in inspirational talk radio featuring top Hay House authors! And, sign up via the Hay House USA Website to receive the Hay House online newsletter and stay informed about what's going on with your favorite authors. You'll receive bimonthly announcements about Discounts and Offers, Special Events, Product Highlights, Free Excerpts, Giveaways, and more!
www.hayhouse.com®